Financial Literacy
Grades 6–8+

Author: Schyrlet Cameron
Editor: Mary Dieterich
Proofreaders: Alexis Fey and April Hawkins

ISBN 978-1-62223-909-2

Printing No. CD-405095

Mark Twain Media, Inc., Publishers
Distributed by Carson Dellosa Education

Visit us at www.marktwainpublishing.com

Table of Contents

Introduction

Financial Literacy is designed to help students in grades six through eight and beyond better understand how the American economic system works. It focuses on five basic principles: debt, budgeting, saving, taxes, and investing. Gaining a basic understanding of how the financial world works and developing essential money management skills will help students make smart financial decisions in the future.

How the Book is Organized

Financial Literacy covers five units of study: Financial vs. Economic Literacy, Making Financial Decisions, The Economy, Taxes, and Money Management. Each of the 18 lessons supports state and national standards. Real-life activities allow students to explore, understand, and apply concepts such as budgeting, saving, borrowing, and investing. This results in meaningful learning that promotes financial literacy. Each lesson contains the following sections:

- **Reading Selection** introduces students to a specific financial concept while building vocabulary.
- **Assessment** evaluates student comprehension of information in the reading selection.
- **Knowledge Builders** are challenging activities that reinforce learning of core financial concepts.

Financial vs. Economic Literacy

Money is an important part of our lives. Knowing how to handle money wisely will help build a secure future.

What Is Financial Literacy?

Financial literacy is understanding and effectively using money management skills. This is important when making economic decisions, such as when to spend, save, and invest. Money management skills include understanding:

- **Debt:** money you spend that isn't yours
- **Saving:** money you set aside for future use
- **Budgeting:** planning and managing your money
- **Investing:** putting your money into something that will make a profit over time
- **Taxes:** money you are required to pay to the government to fund public services

What Is Economic Literacy?

Your financial choices make an impact on the economy. When you spend money, you are participating in the economy. Understanding production, supplying, buying, selling, and the consumption of goods and services are important economic literacy skills.

Economics is the study of how things are bought and sold. Each country has a method of producing items people need and want. An **economy** is the way in which the things people want and need are made, sold, and used in a country. When your parents buy a new house, they participate in the national economy. When you purchase something made in another country, you participate in the global economy.

Goods and services are the products that satisfy our needs and wants. **Goods** are any items that can be bought or sold. Some examples of goods are clothing and computers. **Services** are any actions one person or group does for another in exchange for payment. Some people who provide services include teachers, cooks, and bankers.

Each region of the United States produces goods and services depending on the available resources. A **resource** is anything used to produce goods and services. For example, Washington is one of the top-ranked states in apple production. Its soil, a natural resource, is suitable for growing apples. **Production** is the process of changing raw materials into economic goods that can be used to satisfy the needs and wants of consumers.

Scarcity means we can never have all we want of every good and service. The scarcity of resources includes money and time. Desires and wants for goods and services are unlimited, while resources needed to produce them are limited. People make economic decisions based on the most effective use of their resources.

Name: ______________________________ Date: ____________________

Assessment

Directions: Complete the page using information from the reading selection.

Matching

_____ 1. global economy
_____ 2. financial literacy
_____ 3. resource
_____ 4. services
_____ 5. goods

A. items that can be bought or sold
B. anything used to produce goods and services
C. any actions that one person or group does for another in exchange for payment
D. world economy
E. understanding and effectively using money management skills

Fill in the Blanks

6. Economics is the study of how things are ______________ and ______________.
7. Goods and services are the ______________ that satisfy our needs and wants.
8. Some people who provide services include ______________, ______________, and ______________.
9. Production is the process of changing ______________ materials into economic goods.
10. Scarcity of resources includes ______________ and ______________.

Constructed Response

In your own words, explain the statement, "Desires and wants for goods and services are unlimited, while resources needed to produce them are limited." Use details from the reading selection to support your answer. Write your answer in the box.

Name: ______________________ Date: ______________

Knowledge Builder

What Is the Difference?

Directions: Explain the difference between the paired terms. Write your answer in each box.

1.

National Economy	What Is the Difference?	Global Economy

2.

Financial Literacy	What Is the Difference?	Economic Literacy

3.

Saving	What Is the Difference?	Investing

United States Money

Money is crucial to our lives. We work hard for the money we earn. We spend it on things we need or want, save it for future use, and invest it to make it grow.

Functions of Money

Money has three main functions. First, it is used as a **medium of exchange**, meaning people accept it in exchange for goods or services. Second, it can be used as a **unit of accounting**, which allows people to use it to keep records. Third, it has a **store of value**, meaning people can save it for future purchases.

Currency

The United States **currency** consists of coins and paper money. The United States Mint and the Bureau of Engraving and Printing produce our currency.

Every coin used for buying and selling in the United States is produced by the **United States Mint**. Coins are made of copper, nickel, and an **alloy**, which is a mixture of metals. Coins are **minted**, or manufactured, in six different **denominations**, or amounts. The denominations are penny, nickel, dime, quarter, half dollar, and dollar.

The Bureau of Engraving and Printing designs and produces **Federal Reserve Notes** (paper money). The notes are composed of 25 percent linen and 75 percent cotton. The bills are printed with green ink made from a secret formula to protect against counterfeiting. Bills are issued in the amounts of $1, $2, $5, $10, $20, $50, and $100. Currently, every bill in circulation features pictures of a man who played an important role in the history of the United States. In 2030, Harriet Tubman is scheduled to replace Andrew Jackson on the $20 bill.

Counterfeiting

The currency of the United States has undergone several changes in appearance since the first paper money was issued during the American Revolutionary War. Recently, the $5, $10, $20, $50, and $100 bills have been redesigned. Because of their high value, several security features have been incorporated into the design of these bills. **The Secret Service** is the agency that investigates crimes involving **counterfeiting**, or illegal copying and printing of United States money.

Security Feature	Description
Color-shifting ink	The numeral on the lower right corner changes color when the bill is tilted back and forth.
Watermark	When the bill is held up to the light, another portrait of the person featured on the bill is visible.
Security thread	A thread embedded in the bill glows when held under an ultraviolet light.
Microprinting	The words "The United States of America" are printed so small they are hard to replicate.
Fine-line printing	Selected areas of the bill contain very thin lines incorporated in the design.

Name: ______________________________ Date: ____________________

Assessment

Directions: Complete the page using information from the reading selection.

Matching

_____	1. counterfeiting	A.	agency that investigates crimes of counterfeiting
_____	2. unit of accounting	B.	accepted in exchange for goods or services
_____	3. Secret Service	C.	can be saved for future purchases
_____	4. medium of exchange	D.	illegally reproducing money for circulation
_____	5. store of value	E.	can be used in the keeping of records

True or False

Write *T* if the statement is true. Write *F* if the statement is false. If the statement is false, rewrite the answer below the statement to make it true.

_____ 6. The United States currency is made up of coins and paper money.

_____ 7. The United States Mint produces coin and bills.

_____ 8. The $1,000 bill is the largest bill printed in the United States.

_____ 9. Copying and printing of United States money is illegal.

_____ 10. The first U.S. paper money was issued during the Civil War.

Constructed Response

An embedded (not printed) security thread is added to all bills except the $1 and $2 bills. Why do you think only larger bills have the security thread? Use details from the reading selection to support your answer. Write your answer in the box.

Name: ______________________________ Date: ____________________

Knowledge Builder

United States Coins

Directions: Use reference sources or the Internet to complete the following research project. Next to each denomination, state the famous figure engraved on the coin and the illustration found on the reverse side. Include the year of the coin you are researching. (Reverse illustrations may vary on some coins due to the year or program being featured by the U.S. Mint.)

Denomination	Famous Figure	Reverse Illustration/Year
1. Penny 		
2. Nickel 		
3. Dime 		
4. Quarter 		
5. Half Dollar 		

Name: ______________________________ Date: ____________________

Knowledge Builder

United States Bills

Directions: Use reference sources or the Internet to complete the following research project. Next to each denomination, state the famous figure printed on the bill and the illustration found on the reverse side of each bill for the current year.

Denomination	Famous Figure	Reverse Illustration
1. 		
2. 		
3. 		
4. 		
5. 		
6. 		

Name: ______________________ Date: ______________

Knowledge Builder

Security Features

Directions: Gather a five-, ten-, and twenty-dollar bill. Examine the security features on each bill and complete the table. Use a magnifying glass to locate microprinting and fine-line printing. Use ultraviolet light to discover the location and color of the security threads.

Bills	FIVE 5 FIVE	TEN 10 TEN	TWENTY 20 TWENTY
1. Date of Issue			
2. Color of Security Thread			
3. Location of Security Thread			
4. Color of Shifting Ink			
5. Words on Security Thread			
6. Words Used in Microprinting			
7. Location of Microprinting			
8. Person Featured on Bill			
9. Watermark	yes/no	yes/no	yes/no
10. Serial Number			

Money Math

When you go to the grocery store, you can tell the cost of an item by the price tag. The price is represented with a decimal number.

Money as a Decimal

Money is written as a decimal number. The amount is written using the dollar sign ($) and a decimal point (.).

Number of Dollars

↓

Dollar Sign → **$4.95** ← **Number of cents**

↑

Decimal point (and)

We read the number as
"four dollars and ninety-five cents."

Dollars and Cents

The dollar bill is the basic unit of money in the United States. The dollar equals 100 one-cent coins, or pennies. You can write the number of cents by writing the coin's value and adding a cent sign (¢). For example, 1¢, 10¢, or 25¢. The amount can also be written as a decimal.

100 Cents in 1 Dollar

One dollar equals 100 cents.
The cent amount is written after the decimal point.
A zero (0) is used as a place holder.

1 cent	= $0.01
10 cents	= $0.10
1 dollar	= $1.00
1 dollar and 1 cent	= $1.01
1 dollar and 10 cents	= $1.10

Money Math (cont.)

How to Add and Subtract Decimals

Adding Decimals

Equation: \$5.60 + \$6.32 =

$$\begin{array}{r} 5.60 \\ +\ 6.32 \\ \hline \$11.92 \end{array}$$

Steps:

1. Write the equation vertically and line up the decimal points.
2. Add as you would with whole numbers.
3. Move the decimal point straight down into the answer.

Subtracting Decimals

Equation: \$43.94 – \$2.02 =

$$\begin{array}{r} 8\ 10 \\ 43.90 \\ -\ 2.02 \\ \hline \$41.88 \end{array}$$

Steps:

1. Write the equation vertically and line up the decimal points.
2. Subtract as you would with whole numbers.
3. Move the decimal point straight down into the answer.

How to Multiply and Divide Decimals

Multiplying Decimals

Equation: \$2.80 x 3 =

$$\begin{array}{rr} 2.80 & 2\text{ digits} \\ \times\ 3 & +\,0\text{ digits} \\ \hline \$8.40 & 2\text{ digits} \end{array}$$

Steps:

1. Write the equation vertically.
2. Multiply as you do with whole numbers.
3. Count the number of digits to the right of the decimal places in the problem. Place the same number of digits after the decimal point in the answer.

Dividing Decimals

Equation: \$5.00 ÷ 4 =

$$\begin{array}{r} \$1.25 \\ 4\,\overline{)\,5.00} \\ -\,4 \\ \hline 1\,0 \\ -\,8 \\ \hline 2\,0 \\ -\,20 \\ \hline 0 \end{array}$$

Steps:

1. Write the equation inside a long division bracket.
2. Place the decimal point directly above the decimal point in the division bracket
3. Divide as you do with whole numbers.

Name: ______________________ Date: ______________

Assessment

Directions: Fill in the bubble next to the correct answer for each multiple-choice question.

1. \$8.36 + \$0.73 =
   - ❍ A. \$8.63
   - ❍ B. \$7.63
   - ❍ C. \$9.09
   - ❍ D. \$9.63

2. \$6.70 x 3 =
   - ❍ A. \$2.01
   - ❍ B. \$20.10
   - ❍ C. \$18.10
   - ❍ D. \$18.20

3. \$7.03 – \$3.26 =
   - ❍ A. \$3.77
   - ❍ B. \$4.77
   - ❍ C. \$3.76
   - ❍ D. \$4.76

4. \$41.50 ÷ 10 =
   - ❍ A. \$4.10
   - ❍ B. \$4.00
   - ❍ C. \$4.15
   - ❍ D. \$4.50

Directions: Complete each problem. Show your work.

5. Ted has \$5.85. He lends \$2.90 to Steve and \$1.25 to Stefanie. How much does he have left?	6. Tara is saving to buy a membership to the local amusement park. The membership fee is \$38.50. She has 10 weeks in which to save for the membership. How much money should she save each week?

Budgeting

A **budget** is a plan for spending your money. It helps you decide how much to spend and how much to save. Creating a budget and sticking to it can help you spend your money wisely and save for the future.

Money Management

Money is used to buy things you need and want. **Needs** are things you need to survive, such as food. **Wants** are things you would like to have but are not needed for survival, like a bicycle. Understanding the difference between the two can help you prioritize your spending. When you understand how you spend your money, you can better manage your monthly expenses. Good money management will allow you to save and achieve goals, such as buying a car or going on a trip.

Steps for Making a Budget

To create your budget, you should first determine your income. **Income** is the money that you receive regularly, such as allowance or money earned from doing chores, babysitting, or part-time jobs. Next, track spending by figuring out your **expenses**, or where your money is going. There are two types of expenses: fixed expenses and variable expenses. **Fixed expenses** stay the same from month-to-month and include rent and car payments. **Variable expenses** are costs that can change from month-to-month, such as groceries and entertainment. The last step is making sure you are staying on budget. This may require you to reduce spending for variable expenses to ensure you have enough money to pay all fixed monthly expenses.

The 50/30/20 Budget Rule

The 50/30/20 rule is a way to organize your spending. It is a budgeting guideline that suggests dividing your income into three groups.

- First: 50% of your income should go to your needs—essential expenses like rent, utilities, groceries, transportation costs, and any bills you need to pay.
- Second: 30% of your income should go to your wants—fun stuff like eating out, entertainment, hobbies, and travel.
- Third: 20% of your income should go to savings and debt repayment, such as putting money aside for retirement and credit card debt.

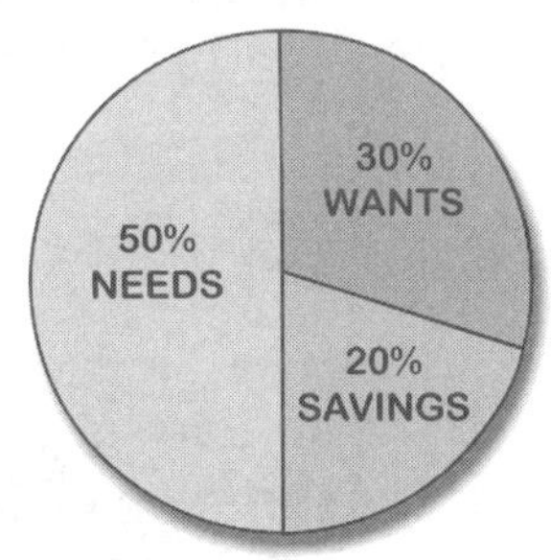

Calculating Your 50/30/20 Budget

Dividing your income based on the 50/30/20 budget plan is not difficult. There is an easy way. First, convert the percentage to a decimal. Next, multiply income by each of the decimals.

Example: Income is $200.

	Needs	Wants	Savings
Step 1:	50% = 50. = 0.50	30% = 30. = 0.30	20% = 20. = 0.20
Step 2:	$200 x 0.50 = $100	$200 x 0.30 = $60	$200 x 0.20 = $40

Name: ______________________________ Date: ______________________

Assessment

Directions: Answer the following questions. Use details from the reading selection to support your answers.

1. What is a budget?

2. Money is for buying the things we need and want. Explain the difference between needs and wants, and give an example of each.

3. A budget should be made with the idea that it can change at any time. Explain what might cause someone to have to adjust their budget.

4. Fixed expenses are the costs that occur regularly every month. They do not usually change from month to month. What are two examples of fixed expenses?

5. Variable expenses are the costs that change from month to month. What are two examples of variable expenses?

6. Your income is $100 for the month. Based on the 50/30/20 budget rule, answer the following questions:
   - What is the dollar amount you should budget for needs? ______________
   - What is the dollar amount you should budget for wants? ______________
   - What is the dollar amount you should budget for savings? ______________

Name: ______________________ Date: ______________________

Knowledge Builder

Financial Needs and Wants

Directions: Complete the page.

1. What are needs?

2. What are wants?

5. List five of your financial needs.

   1. ______________
   2. ______________
   3. ______________
   4. ______________
   5. ______________

3. Why is it important to understand the difference between wants and needs when creating a budget? Explain.

6. List five of your financial wants.

   1. ______________
   2. ______________
   3. ______________
   4. ______________
   5. ______________

4. If you only had enough money in your budget for one thing, would it be better to choose a need or a want? Explain.

Name: ______________________ Date: ______________________

Knowledge Builder

50/30/20 Budget Rule

Directions: At the beginning of the month, use the 50/30/20 rule to create a budget based on your estimated monthly income. At the end of the month, complete the Budget Summary and Budget Evaluation sections of the activity.

Estimated Monthly Income	Amount
Allowance	
Chores	
Babysitting	
Part-time Job	
Other	
Total	

50% Essential Spending (needs)	Amount
School supplies	
Transportation	
Other	
Total	

30% Discretionary Spending (wants)	Amount
Entertainment	
Snacks	
Other	
Total	

20% Financial Goals (savings, investing, emergency, debt)	Amount
Savings	
Emergencies	
Other	
Total	

My 50/30/20 Plan

Divide your total monthly income using the 50/30/20 rule. This will let you know the amount you can spend for your needs, wants, and goals for the month.

Total Income ______________

50% ______________

30% ______________

20% ______________

Budget Evaluation

Did you stay within your budget?

What could you do to improve your monthly spending?

Budget Summary	Amount Budgeted	Actual Amount
Monthly Income		
Essential Spending		
Discretionary Spending		
Financial Goals		
Total		

Smart Shopping

Shopping is buying goods or services from a **retailer**, or seller. People shop in many ways including online, in stores, through catalogs, and through door-to-door sales. Smart shopping can help you avoid making mistakes with your money.

Shopping List

It is a good idea to make a list of what you need before shopping. Without a list, you can easily make the mistake of buying things that you don't actually need and did not plan to purchase.

Impulse buying is an unplanned purchase. Stores encourage impulse buying to increase sales, such as placing candy displays next to the checkout lane. When tempted to make an impulse purchase, wait 24 hours to think it over.

Comparison Shopping

Sometimes, different stores sell the same item or similar items. Taking the time to shop around and compare prices from different retailers can help you save money.

Some stores use unit pricing to help consumers compare grocery items packaged in different amounts. Unit prices are usually posted on the shelf where the product is located. But if not, unit prices are easy to calculate. To determine the unit price, divide the cost of the item by the number of ounces, or units, it contains.

Example: Fresh Mart Milk $4.49 ÷ 32 oz = $0.14 per ounce
Shop Right Milk $4.07 ÷ 32 oz = $0.13 per ounce

Shop Right milk is the best buy.

Online Shopping

Online shopping has made buying the things we need and want more convenient. Shoppers can research different stores and websites to find the best price for an item they are interested in purchasing. However, it's important to know how to shop safely to avoid online scams. You will probably have to pay with a credit card, so make sure the site offers secure information transfer. The following tips can help you avoid scams when shopping online.

Online Shopping Tips

- Sticking to retail sites you know and trust is one of the best ways to avoid scams.
- Check for the lock icon when visiting a website. This indicates the site is secure.
- Check the URL to ensure a website is secure; HTTPS is secure, but HTTP is not secure. The extra "s" in HTTPS stands for *secure*.
- Check the URL for misspellings or missing letters, such as .co instead of .com.
- Check reviews from other customers who have purchased the item. The review informs potential buyers of the benefits and downsides of a specific product.

Name: ______________________________ Date: ______________________

Assessment

Directions: Compare the prices of the different brands of baby food below. Find the best price by calculating the unit price for each brand and choosing the least expensive.

Brand	Price per Jar	Ounces per Jar	Price per Ounce
1. Cute Baby	$1.99	3 oz.	
2. Best Buy	$2.09	4 oz.	
3. Yum-Yum	$1.79	2 oz.	

4. What is the least expensive brand? ____________________

Constructed Response

Dan was searching the Internet for the Dog Paw website to order a chew toy for his dog. Explain why the website address he found is not secure and may be a scam. Use details from the reading selection to support your answer. Write your answer in the box.

Name: ______________________ Date: ______________

Knowledge Builder

Comparison Grocery Shopping

Directions: List five food items. Check the brand name price and store brand price for each item at the supermarket. Record the prices.

Brand Name Price	Food Item	Store Brand Price
$ ________	________	$ ________
$ ________	________	$ ________
$ ________	________	$ ________
$ ________	________	$ ________
$ ________	________	$ ________

Which brand has the lowest prices? ________________

Directions: You are going grocery shopping. To complete the table, start by listing five food items. Include brand name and size. Check the prices of these items at two different stores. Record the prices.

Food Item	Brand Name	Size	Store 1 Price	Store 2 Price

Store 1 total = $ ________ Store 2 total = $ ________

Which store should you shop at for the lowest prices? ________________

Name: ______________________________ Date: ____________________

Knowledge Builder

Shopping on the Internet

Directions: Complete the table. Select an item that you would like to purchase. Find two sites on the Internet where you can buy this item. Compare the information.

Shopping on the Internet		
Product: ______________________________		
Name	**Company A**	**Company B**
Website Address		
Price		
Credit Card Fees		
Guarantee		
Return and Refund Policies		
Customer Service and Support (Telephone Number and Contact Information)		
A Customer Review or Recommendation		
Shipping Charge		

Which company is the best option for purchasing the item? ____________________

Discounts and Coupons

Sales promotions such as discounts and coupons are ways businesses encourage you to buy their products.

Sales and Discounts

Sales and discounts are a way for shoppers to save money. When the regular price of an item or service is lowered, it is called a **sales discount**. The **sale price** is how much a customer will pay for an item after the discount is subtracted. A sales discount is often listed as a percentage such as 10%, 25% or 50%. To figure out the price of the item after the discount is easy.

Example: 25% discount on a book that costs \$5.99 = \$1.50

How to Calculate Sale Price After Discount	
Step 1: Convert percent to a decimal	25% = 25 = 25. = .25 = 0.25
Step 2: Multiply price by discount	5.99 x 0.25 = 1.4975
Step 3: Round answer to nearest hundredth of a dollar	1.4975 = \$1.50
Step 2: Subtract discount amount from the price of item	\$5.99 – \$1.50 = \$4.49 **Sale price** is \$4.49

Coupons and Discount Codes

Coupons and discount codes can be used to redeem special discounts and deals, in-store or online. A **coupon** is a small piece of paper that allows you to get a service or product for free or at a lower price. Coupons are also available online. A **promotional code**, or discount code, is made up of random letters and numbers that often appear on coupons or retailers' websites. When the code is entered at checkout, the discount is applied to the price.

Sales Discounts as Fractions

Fractions are often used to offer discounts. An easy method for finding the discount is to divide the price of an item by the fraction's denominator.

Example: A box of cereal costs \$3.00.
How much will it cost with a ½ off coupon?

Step 1: Divide sales price by discount:
\$3.00 ÷ 2 = \$1.50

Step 2: Subtract discount from sales price:
\$3.00 – \$1.50 = \$1.50
Sale price is \$1.50.

Fraction Discount		
Fourth	Third	Half
1/4	1/3	1/2
÷ by 4	÷ by 3	÷ by 2

Name: ______________________________ Date: ____________________

Assessment

Directions: Write *T* if the statement is true. Write *F* if the statement is false. If the statement is false, rewrite the answer below the statement to make it true.

____ 1. The sales discount is how much a customer will pay for an item after the discount is subtracted.

____ 2. Coupons are ways businesses encourage you to buy their products.

Directions: Calculate each sales discount and sale price. Round your answers to the nearest hundredth (to the nearest cent). Show your work.

3. A book normally costs \$8.00. How much will it cost if a 15% coupon is used for the purchase?	4. A pair of sunglasses is normally \$15.00. It is now on sale for 1/3 off. What will the sale price be with the discount?

Constructed Response

Explain the differences between coupons and discount codes. Use details from the reading selection to support your answer. Write your answer in the box.

Name: ______________________________ Date: ______________________

Knowledge Builder

Coupon Shopping

Directions: Complete the table and answer the questions below. Make a grocery list. Visit the store's website and apps, check your local Sunday newspaper, and pick up weekly ads at stores to find coupons or promotional codes for as many of the items on your list as you can. In the table below, include item name, regular price, coupon discount, and price of item with discount. Make sure to check coupon specifications for minimum purchase requirements, usage restrictions, and customer eligibility.

Grocery List				
Grocery Item	**Regular Price**	**Coupon Discount**	**Coupon Specifications**	**Price with Discount**
1.				
2.				
3.				
4.				
5.				

6. What is the total of the five items with the regular store price? ____________________
7. What is the total of the five items with the discount? ____________________
8. How much money would you save using the coupons? ____________________
9. In your opinion, is using coupons worth the time and effort? Explain. ____________________

____

____

Name: ______________________________ Date: ____________________

Knowledge Builder

Sales Discount Codes

Directions: Collect four coupons with promo codes. Visit the store's website or check your local newspaper for coupons. Make sure to check coupon specifications for minimum purchase requirements, usage restrictions, and customer eligibility. Use the coupons to complete the activity.

Sales Discount Code

Store: ____________________

Item: ____________________

Code: ____________________

Discount: ____________________

Expiration Date: ____________________

Specifications:

Sales Discount Code

Store: ____________________

Item: ____________________

Code: ____________________

Discount: ____________________

Expiration Date: ____________________

Specifications:

Sales Discount Code

Store: ____________________

Item: ____________________

Code: ____________________

Discount: ____________________

Expiration Date: ____________________

Specifications:

Sales Discount Code

Store: ____________________

Item: ____________________

Code: ____________________

Discount: ____________________

Expiration Date: ____________________

Specifications:

Sales Receipts

A **sales receipt** is issued by the store when you make a purchase. Without the original receipt, you cannot prove that you paid for the items. Stores require the customer present the original receipt to exchange the item or receive a refund.

Receipt Information

The sales receipt contains important details about the purchase, including

- **Store Details:** name, address, phone number and/or email address
- **Transaction Details:** date, month, and year
- **Product Details:** item code, product description, quantity sold, and price
- **Payment Details:** total, taxes, tip, discounts, and payment method
- **Important Message:** return policy, instructions, promotional message, and barcode

Main Street Market
(412) 555-0172
Manager Kim Reynolds
1405 Main Street
Reed Springs, MO 65737

01/03/2024 11:59 Cashier: Lee Smith

1678 Notebook	1	$4.95
4092 Pkg Pencils	1	$2.95
	Subtotal	$7.90
	Sales Tax	$0.67
	Total	$8.57
	Cash	$10.00
	Change	$1.43

Exchange & refund within 14 days with original receipt

State Sales Tax

State sales tax is a fee added to the price of a purchase or service. The purpose of a sales tax is to raise money for the local government. The money is used to pay for things like building and maintaining roads, police and fire departments, and schools.

Each state has its own sales tax charge, or rate. Cities and counties may also impose local sales taxes as well. The sales tax increases the total amount of a purchase. The amount of tax charged for a purchase depends on the combined state and local rate at the location of the purchase. Food and medicine may be taxed at one rate, and other items, such as clothing and cell phones, at a different rate.

Tipping

A **tip**, or **gratuity**, is a small amount of money given voluntarily to someone serving you, such as a waiter or barber. A tip is a way of thanking people for good service. Tips depend on the service.

- 15% for average service
- 18% for good service
- Above 20% for excellent service
- For poor service: talk to the manager

Most people prefer a cash tip. Some businesses have a digital display screen where you can select your tip. Others automatically add the gratuity to the sales receipt.

Note: Tips and discounts are figured on the subtotal before taxes are added.

Subtotal:	$50.00
Sales Tax:	$3.64
Gratuity:	$7.50
Amt Due:	$61.14

THANK YOU!

15% tip would be $7.50
18% tip would be $9.00
20% tip would be $10.00

Name: ______________________ Date: ______________________

Assessment

Directions: Fill in the bubble next to the correct answer for each multiple-choice question.

1. A gratuity is
   - ❍ A. required.
   - ❍ B. given voluntarily.
   - ❍ C. a tax.
   - ❍ D. a discount.

2. A sales receipt
   - ❍ A. is a coupon.
   - ❍ B. is a small amount of money.
   - ❍ C. represents proof of purchase.
   - ❍ D. is a gift card for later use.

3. Sales tax on a store receipt is
   - ❍ A. a discount.
   - ❍ B. given voluntarily.
   - ❍ C. a tip.
   - ❍ D. an added fee.

4. The tax rate charged for a purchase depends on
   - ❍ A. the store.
   - ❍ B. the customer.
   - ❍ C. the location of the purchase.
   - ❍ D. the price of items purchased.

Directions: Complete each problem.

5. What is the subtotal after the discount and the total cost of the purchase?

Subtotal	$45.44
Discount	$5.00
Subtotal	$________
Sales Tax 6.00%	$2.43
Total	$________

6. Calculate the total and change back for the purchase.

Subtotal	$30.00
Sales Tax 5.25%	$1.58
Gratuity 15%	$4.50
Total	$________
Cash	$50.00
Change	$________

Name: ______________________ Date: ______________________

Knowledge Builder

Sales Receipts

Directions: Use the sales receipt to fill in the blanks.

Store Details

1. Name ______________________
2. Address ______________________

   ____
3. Store manager ______________________
4. Store cashier ______________________
5. Phone number and/or email address

   ____

Transaction Details

6. Date and time ______________________

Product Details

7. Item code ______________________
8. Product description ______________________
9. Quantity sold ______________________
10. Price each ______________________

Payment Details

11. Subtotal ______________________
12. Discounts ______________________
13. Taxes ______________________
14. Total ______________________
15. Payment method ______________________

Important Message

16. Promotional code ______________________
17. Return & refund instructions ______________________

    ____

Sports and More
(615) 555-0109
Manager Sam West
405 East Street
Greenfield, NY 12833

07/22/2024 1:59 Cashier: Kate Jones

2678 T-shirt 2 @ $22.72

Subtotal	$45.44
Discount	$5.00
Sales Tax 6.00%	$2.43
Total	$42.87
Credit Card	$42.87

Valid: Monday, September 10 through Sunday, September 24
Promo Code: 45AV182

TO REDEEM IN-STORE SHOW BARCODE TO CASHIER

Exchange & refund within 10 days with original receipt.

THANK YOU!

Name: ______________________ Date: ______________

Knowledge Builder

Tipping Guide

Directions: Use the Tipping Guide to complete each activity.

How to Calculate Tips

To calculate a tip, multiply the price of the purchases before taxes by the percentage of the tip. Answers are rounded to the nearest tenth of a cent.

Example: The bill is $25.00. How much is a 15% tip? $25.00 x 0.15 = $3.75

Tipping Guide

15% (0.15) = Average Service

18% (0.18) = Good Service

20% (0.20) = Excellent Service

Directions: Fill in the blanks. You had lunch at the Hamburger Palace. The service was excellent.

Hamburger Palace
(565) 555-0180
Manager Clarissa Williams
105 Main Street
Westport, OR 97016

08/12/2024 4:09 Server: Tom Hall

Cheeseburger	$15.00
Fries	$3.95
Subtotal	$ ______
Sales Tax	$1.68
Total	$ ______
Credit Card	#####2091

Suggested Tips

15% (Tip $ ______ Total $ ______)
18% (Tip $ ______ Total $ ______)
20% (Tip $ ______ Total $ ______)

Tip $ ______
Total $ ______

X ______________________
SIGNATURE

Directions: Fill in the blanks and answer the question below for the receipt from Pizza Delight.

PIZZA DELIGHT
(212) 555-0124
Manager Lou Evans
905 North Street
Miller, MO 65707

10/02/2024 6:49 Server: Alice Hart
Table: 10

2 Deluxe Pizzas	$35.76
4 Soda Drinks	$18.00
2 Salads	$15.00
2 Ice Cream Cones	$5.50
Subtotal	$ ______
Sales Tax 4.22%	$3.13
Total	$ ______
Cash	$100.00
Change	$ ______

The service was average. How much tip should you leave? ______________

Ups and Downs in the Economy

"Good times" and "hard times" are phrases often used to describe the ups and downs in the U.S. economy. When the economy is growing, businesses increase production, work is plentiful, and people have money to spend. This economic growth leads to a time of financial prosperity. However, this period of growth will not last forever because competition for goods and services causes **inflation**, or an increase in prices. People are forced to pay more for goods and services, so they are able to buy less. When the economy finally slows down, people spend less money, companies cut back on production, and workers are laid off. Some businesses may fail or close. The economy then enters a period of decline in business activity. Eventually, the economy will pick up, and the cycle begins again.

Phases of the Economic Cycle

Expansion is a time when business is booming. New businesses are opening. There are lots of jobs for people, wages are high, and the unemployment rate is low. People have extra money; they buy new houses and new cars, go on trips to other countries, and invest in the stock market. People can borrow money from banks at low **interest rates**, or fees, because they have a steady income.

Slowdown is a time when businesses are still operating in a healthy way but stop hiring new employees. Slowly, the banks start increasing the interest rates on loans. People start to think twice about buying a house or a new car. The prices of some items in the grocery store begin to increase. The price of stock on the stock market begins to drop. People begin to be cautious about spending money.

A **recession** usually occurs when some major event happens, such as a stock market crash, a war, a major pandemic, or a natural catastrophe like a hurricane or drought. The interest on bank loans skyrockets. Businesses can't sell their products because people are afraid to spend money. They start to lay off their workers and close their doors. People lose their homes because they are no longer employed. If the recession lasts too long, it can become a **depression**.

Recovery is the time it takes for a country to come out of a recession or depression. Usually, the government initiates programs to help individuals and companies start again, and slowly, people start to find jobs. The government can also pay some employees' salaries to encourage companies to hire. The banks are forced to lower the interest rates on loans.

Controlling the Economy

The government continuously monitors and regulates the economy. When the economy is expanding, the government tries to slow down spending by people and businesses. To do this, the government might raise taxes or interest rates and cut government spending. To combat inflation, people are encouraged to spend less and save more, while businesses are encouraged to produce more to decrease prices. During a recession or depression, the government tries to increase the amount of money in the economy, so people and businesses have more to spend. They might cut taxes, lower interest rates, or increase government spending on public works to keep companies and businesses producing and workers employed.

Name: ______________________________ Date: ____________________

Assessment

Directions: Complete this page using information from the reading selection.

Matching

_____ 1. economic cycle
_____ 2. recession
_____ 3. depression
_____ 4. inflation
_____ 5. expansion

A. increase in prices due to competition for goods and services
B. recession that continues for too long
C. decline in business activity
D. economic growth
E. the continuous sequence of ups and downs in the economy

Fill in the Blanks

6. When the economy is ________________, businesses increase production, work is plentiful, and people have money to spend.
7. Competition for goods and services causes ________________.
8. When the economy is ________________, the government tries to slow down spending by people and businesses.
9. To combat inflation, people are encouraged to spend ________________ and ________________ more.
10. To combat inflation, businesses are encouraged to produce more to ________________ prices.

Constructed Response

Explain how inflation can affect your spending power. Use details from the reading selection to support your answer. Write your answer in the box.

Name: ______________________ Date: ______________

Knowledge Builder

Phases of the Economic Cycle

Directions: Explain each phase of the economic cycle. Write your answer in each box.

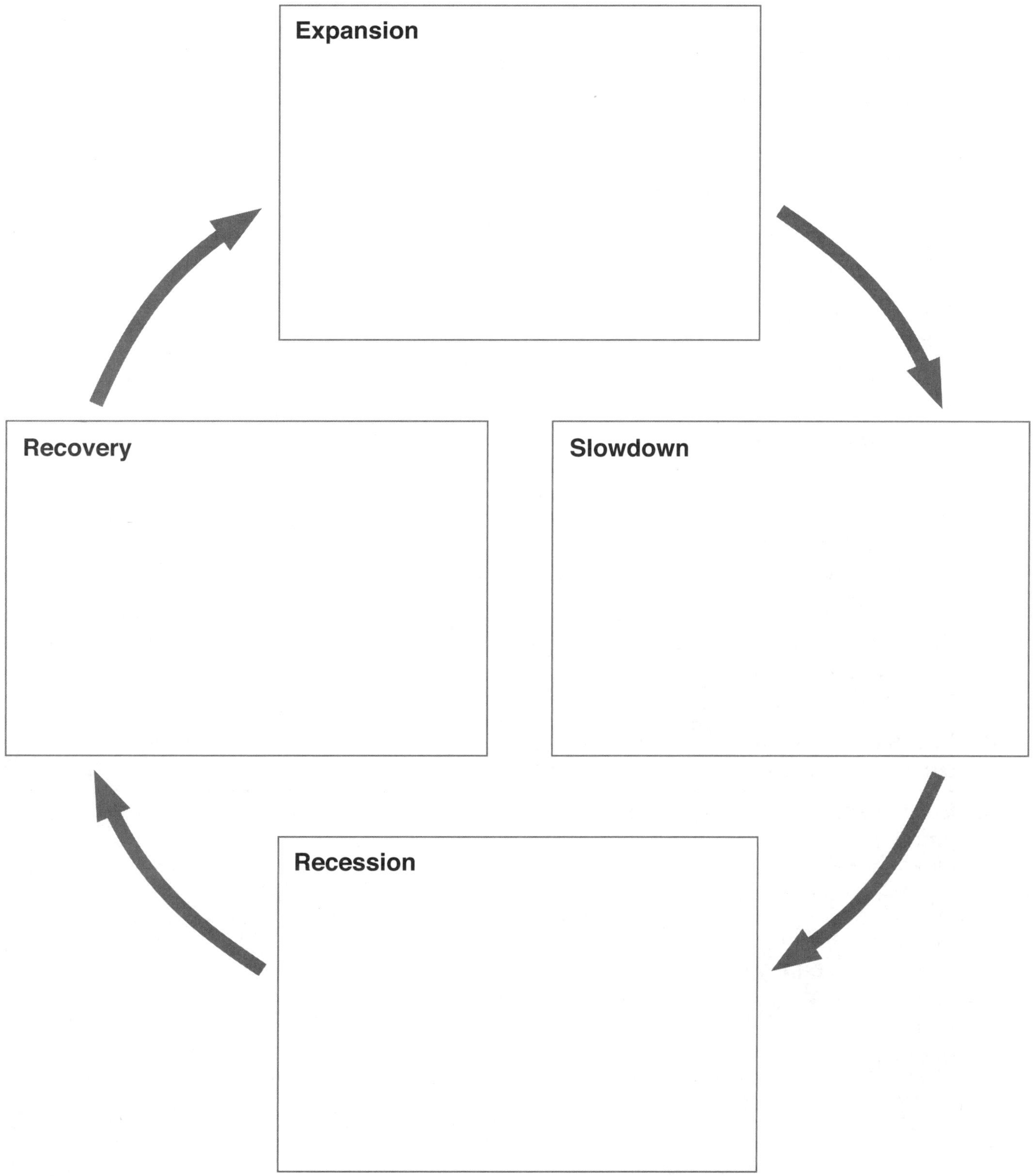

Name: ______________________ Date: ______________

Knowledge Builder

The Economic Cycle

Directions: Read each statement. Place an X in the correct box or boxes for each statement.

Phases of the Economic Cycle				
Statement	**Expansion**	**Slowdown**	**Recession**	**Recovery**
1. Banks lower interest rates on loans.				
2. New businesses are opening.				
3. Interest on bank loans skyrockets.				
4. The government initiates programs to pay for some employees' salaries.				
5. If the phase lasts too long, it can become a depression.				
6. Wages are high and the unemployment rate is low.				
7. Businesses start to lay off workers and to close their doors.				
8. Prices at the grocery store begin to rise.				
9. Businesses increase production, work is plentiful, and people have money to spend.				
10. This is the time it takes for a country to come out of a recession or depression.				

Inflation and Deflation

The costs of goods and services can change over time. Inflation occurs when the prices of goods and services rise too much and too quickly, while deflation occurs when those prices decrease. Both can have an impact on your budget and spending.

Inflation

Inflation means a rise in the price of goods and services. Inflation occurs when goods and services are in high demand, thus creating a drop in supply. Inflation causes money to lose its purchasing power. This means the consumer will pay more for goods like a box of cereal and services like getting a haircut.

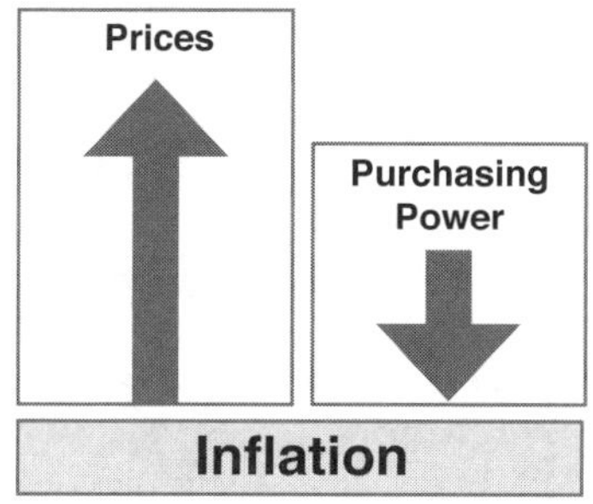

Types of Inflation

Inflation can vary in pace. There are four different types of inflation. The type is based on how quickly the prices of goods and services rise in an economy.

Four Types of Inflation			
Inflation	**Inflation Rate**	**Description**	**Effect**
Creeping Inflation	1% to 3% or less per year	Slow, steady rise in prices	Consumers expect that prices will keep going up, which boosts demand.
Walking Inflation	3% to 10% per year	Fast rise in prices	People begin to buy more than they need to avoid higher prices later.
Galloping Inflation	More than 10% per year	Prices rise quickly	Wages can't keep up with rising costs.
Hyperinflation	50% or more per month	Inflation is out of control	This rarely happens, but when it does, the prices of goods and services increase sharply.

Deflation

Deflation is the opposite of inflation. It is a decrease in the price of goods and services. Deflation occurs when too many goods and services are available or when there is not enough money circulating to purchase those goods or pay for the services. As a result, prices drop. For instance, if a particular type of car becomes highly popular, other manufacturers start to make a similar car to compete. Eventually, car companies will have more of that car style than they can sell, so they must drop the price to attract buyers. Soon, car companies cut costs, which often leads to workers being laid off. People without jobs do not have enough money to buy cars. Car companies lower prices more, which continues the downward cycle.

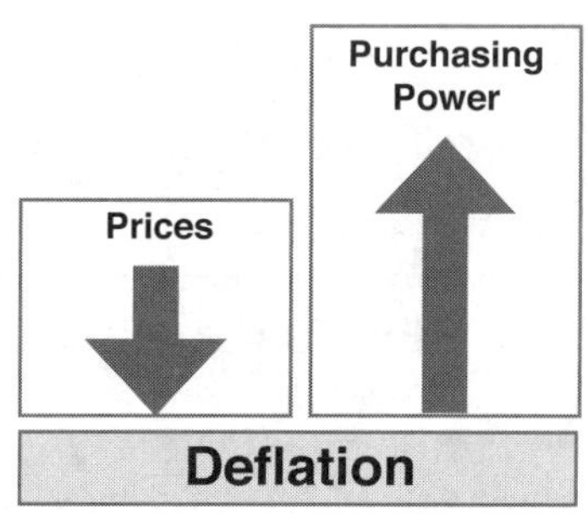

Name: ______________________________ Date: ______________________

Assessment

Directions: Answer the following questions in complete sentences. Use details from the reading selection to support your answers.

1. Why is there an increase in production during inflation?

2. Why is there a decrease in production during deflation?

3. Why are people living on retirement incomes hit hardest during periods of inflation?

4. Which type of inflation is most likely to be beneficial for an economy?

5. An inflation rate of 5% would be classified as what type of inflation?

6. What is the effect of galloping inflation on the consumer?

Name: ______________________ Date: ______________

Knowledge Builder

Cost of Real Estate

Directions: Fill in the blanks and answer each question.

No Inflation

Demand = 3 **Supply = 3**

In this economy, the demand for houses is equal to the supply of houses (number of houses for sale). The cost of a house remains reasonable.

Inflation

1. Demand = ______________ Supply = ______________
2. Does this economy have too little or too much money? ______________
3. Does this cause the cost of the houses to go up or down? ______________
4. Why? ______________
5. Does this mean the value of the dollar has gone up or down? ______________

Deflation

6. Demand = ______________ Supply = ______________
7. Does this economy have too little or too much money? ______________
8. Does this cause the cost of the houses to go up or down? ______________
9. Why? ______________
10. Does this mean the value of the dollar has gone up or down? ______________

Name: ______________________ Date: ______________

Knowledge Builder

Menu Prices

Directions: Use the menu to answer the questions.

The Deli Mart

Menu Price Change

Item	Old Price	New Price
Grilled Cheese Sandwich	$3.00	$2.90
Ham and Cheese Sandwich	$3.75	$4.50
Turkey Club Sandwich	$4.59	$4.75
Roast Beef Sandwich	$4.25	$4.50
Potato Chips	$1.75	$1.50
French Fries	$1.25	$2.50
Giant Cookie	$1.50	$2.25
Fresh Fruit Cup	$2.50	$2.25
Soda	$1.25	$2.75
Milk	$2.00	$1.90
Lemonade	$2.05	$1.55

"Where your dollar always buys more… good food!"

Questions

1. Which menu items inflated in price? ______________________________
2. Which item inflated the most? ______________________________
3. Which menu items deflated in price? ______________________________
4. Which item deflated the most? ______________________________
5. You ordered a grilled cheese sandwich, potato chips, soda, and a giant cookie.
   How much did your order cost? ______________
   How much would you have paid for the same order using the old prices? ______________
   Was this change an inflation or deflation in price? ______________

Financing the Government

Cities, states, and the federal government all need a source of revenue to pay expenses. Examples of expenses are salaries of elected officials, such as the president, members of Congress, and public employees such as police. The government must pay for public goods and services it provides to citizens. **Public goods and services** include national defense, public health services, libraries, parks, education, and road improvements. The **Internal Revenue Service (IRS)** is a federal agency that collects taxes.

Taxes

Taxes are required payments of money the government collects from individuals and businesses. There are many different types of taxes.

Tax	Collection of Tax	Basis for Tax
Income Tax: a percentage of the money deducted from what a person makes at their job. People complete a W-4 form at the start of any new job. This form tells the employer how much federal income tax to keep from each paycheck. This form is crucial in determining the person's balance due or refund each tax season.	Collected by your employer and sent to a city, a state, and/or the federal government	Based on the yearly earnings of individuals or businesses
Property Tax: a charge on privately owned property, including land and cars. The property owner usually pays the tax yearly.	Collected by the local government	Based on the value of the residential and/or personal property
Sales Tax: a charge added to the price of goods and services.	Collected by a business and sent to the local and/or state government	Based on the price individuals pay for goods and services
Social Security Tax: a payroll tax paid by employers and employees to fund the U.S. Social Security program. It is meant to provide a monthly income for people when they retire.	Collected by your employer and sent to the federal government	Based on monthly wages earned by the worker
Medicare Tax: a payroll tax paid by employers and employees to fund the U.S. Medicare program. It pays to help people age 65 and over who are sick and need medical care.	Collected by your employer and sent to the federal government	Based on monthly wages earned by the worker

Name: ______________________________ Date: ______________________

Assessment

Directions: Complete the page using information from the reading selection.

Matching

_____	1. revenue	A.	provides most of the money the government spends
_____	2. taxes	B.	helps people when they retire
_____	3. public goods and services	C.	provided by the government
_____	4. Social Security tax	D.	a charge added to the price of goods and services
_____	5. sales tax	E.	a source of income

Fill in the Blanks

6. The federal agency that collects taxes in the United States is the ________________ ________________ ________________.
7. ________________ tax is an annual tax you pay for owning a car.
8. ________________ tax is a payroll tax to help people age 65 and over who are sick and need medical care.
9. ________________ tax is a tax that takes a percentage of the money you make at a job.
10. Revenue from the ________________ ________________ tax is used to provide people with a monthly check when they retire.

Constructed Response

Explain how taxes benefit people living in the United States. Use details from the reading selection to support your answer. Write the answer in the box.

Name: ______________________________ Date: ____________________

Knowledge Builder

Job Application Form

Directions: When applying for a job, you will be required to complete a job application form and a W-4 Form. You are applying for a position as an assistant server, or busser, at a restaurant. You will be clearing tables, taking dirty dishes to the dishwasher, setting tables, refilling, and otherwise assisting the waiting staff. The average hourly rate for bussers is $11.59 per hour. Use your personal information to complete the job application form below. If you have no information to enter in a section, write N/A.

<table>
<tr><th colspan="8">Name and Address</th></tr>
<tr><td colspan="4">Name (First, MI, Last)</td><td colspan="4">Social Security Number
000-00-0000</td></tr>
<tr><td colspan="8">Mailing Address</td></tr>
<tr><td colspan="8">City, State, and Zip Code</td></tr>
<tr><td colspan="4">Telephone Number</td><td colspan="4">Alternate Phone</td></tr>
<tr><td colspan="4">If under 18, please list age</td><td colspan="4">Email</td></tr>
<tr><td colspan="8">Marital Status: ________ Single ________ Married</td></tr>
<tr><th colspan="8">Days/Hours Available to Work</th></tr>
<tr><td>☐ I have no preference.</td><td>☐ Mon.</td><td>☐ Tues.</td><td>☐ Wed.</td><td>☐ Thurs.</td><td>☐ Fri.</td><td>☐ Sat.</td><td>☐ Sun.</td></tr>
<tr><td>I am seeking a:</td><td colspan="3">☐ Full-time job</td><td colspan="2">☐ Part-time job</td><td colspan="2">☐ Full or Part-time</td></tr>
<tr><td colspan="4">How many hours can you work weekly?</td><td colspan="2">Can you work nights?</td><td colspan="2">Date available to begin</td></tr>
<tr><th colspan="8">Education</th></tr>
<tr><td colspan="4">School</td><td colspan="2">Location</td><td colspan="2">Years completed</td></tr>
<tr><th colspan="8">Additional Information</th></tr>
<tr><td colspan="6">Have you ever been employed by this organization in the past?</td><td>☐ Yes</td><td>☐ No</td></tr>
<tr><td colspan="6">I certify that I am a U.S. citizen, permanent resident, or a foreign national with authorization to work in the United States.</td><td>☐ Yes</td><td>☐ No</td></tr>
<tr><td colspan="6">Have you ever been convicted of, or entered a plea of guilty, no contest, or had a withheld judgment to a felony?</td><td>☐ Yes</td><td>☐ No</td></tr>
<tr><td colspan="8">If yes, please explain:</td></tr>
</table>

Name: ______________________ Date: ______________

Knowledge Builder (cont.)

Federal Income Tax Form W-4

Directions: Use the information from your job application to complete Form W-4.

Form **W-4**
Department of the Treasury
Internal Revenue Service

Employee's Withholding Certificate

Complete Form W-4 so that your employer can withhold the correct federal income tax from your pay.
Give Form W-4 to your employer.
Your withholding is subject to review by the IRS.

OMB No. 1545-0074

2024

Step 1: Enter Personal Information

(a) First name and middle initial | Last name

(b) Social security number: 000-00-0000

Address

City or town, state, and ZIP code

Does your name match the name on your social security card? If not, to ensure you get credit for your earnings, contact SSA at 800-772-1213 or go to *www.ssa.gov*.

(c) ☐ **Single** or **Married filing separately**
☐ **Married filing jointly** or **Qualifying surviving spouse**
☐ **Head of household** (Check only if you're unmarried and pay more than half the costs of keeping up a home for yourself and a qualifying individual.)

Complete Steps 2–4 ONLY if they apply to you; otherwise, skip to Step 5. See page 2 for more information on each step, who can claim exemption from withholding, and when to use the estimator at *www.irs.gov/W4App*.

Step 2: Multiple Jobs or Spouse Works

Complete this step if you (1) hold more than one job at a time, or (2) are married filing jointly and your spouse also works. The correct amount of withholding depends on income earned from all of these jobs.

Do **only one** of the following.

(a) Use the estimator at *www.irs.gov/W4App* for most accurate withholding for this step (and Steps 3–4). If you or your spouse have self-employment income, use this option; **or**

(b) Use the Multiple Jobs Worksheet on page 3 and enter the result in Step 4(c) below; **or**

(c) If there are only two jobs total, you may check this box. Do the same on Form W-4 for the other job. This option is generally more accurate than (b) if pay at the lower paying job is more than half of the pay at the higher paying job. Otherwise, (b) is more accurate . . . . ☐

Complete Steps 3–4(b) on Form W-4 for only ONE of these jobs. Leave those steps blank for the other jobs. (Your withholding will be most accurate if you complete Steps 3–4(b) on the Form W-4 for the highest paying job.)

Step 3: Claim Dependent and Other Credits

If your total income will be $200,000 or less ($400,000 or less if married filing jointly):

Multiply the number of qualifying children under age 17 by $2,000 $________

Multiply the number of other dependents by $500 . . . . . $________

Add the amounts above for qualifying children and other dependents. You may add to this the amount of any other credits. Enter the total here . . . . **3** $

Step 4 (optional): Other Adjustments

(a) Other income (not from jobs). If you want tax withheld for other income you expect this year that won't have withholding, enter the amount of other income here. This may include interest, dividends, and retirement income . . . . **4(a)** $

(b) Deductions. If you expect to claim deductions other than the standard deduction and want to reduce your withholding, use the Deductions Worksheet on page 3 and enter the result here . . . . **4(b)** $

(c) Extra withholding. Enter any additional tax you want withheld each **pay period** . . **4(c)** $

Step 5: Sign Here

Under penalties of perjury, I declare that this certificate, to the best of my knowledge and belief, is true, correct, and complete.

Employee's signature (This form is not valid unless you sign it.) **Date**

Employers Only

Employer's name and address	First date of employment	Employer identification number (EIN)

For Privacy Act and Paperwork Reduction Act Notice, see page 3. Cat. No. 10220Q Form **W-4** (2024)

Payday

On payday, an employee receives payment for work completed and an **earnings statement**, sometimes referred to as a **pay stub**, that lists earnings and all deductions. Employees can choose to have their pay sent straight to their bank or credit union account electronically or to receive a paycheck. A **paycheck** is a piece of paper that can be exchanged for cash or deposited in the employee's account at a bank.

Wage and Salary

When people work, they provide labor in exchange for income, or pay. Wage and salary are two common ways employees get paid. **Wages** are usually figured by multiplying an hourly pay rate by the number of hours worked. Some wage jobs are restaurant and factory workers. **Salaries** are a fixed amount of pay an employee receives each year. The pay is divided and paid out weekly or monthly. The paycheck tends to be the same amount each payday. Some salary jobs are teachers and physicians.

Minimum wage is the minimum amount an employer can legally pay an employee. The federal minimum wage as of 2024 is $7.25 per hour. Many states have higher minimum wages.

Pay Stub

Employees are given an earnings statement each time they are paid. It is a way for the employee to have a record of how much they earn and the number of deductions they pay. The employer is responsible for deducting, or subtracting, the correct amounts from an employee's earnings and sending them to the correct agencies. City, state, and/or federal government taxes are **mandatory**, or required, deductions. Retirement savings plan contributions and medical, dental, or vision health insurance plans are **voluntary**, or deductions employees choose to have taken from their pay. The employee receives a paycheck for the remaining amount. The following information appears in most earnings statements.

- **YTD (Year-to-Date):** total amount for the current calendar year, up to the present date
- **Gross Pay or Wages:** total amount of money earned during a pay period, before any deductions
- **Rate:** amount paid per hour
- **Hours:** number of hours worked for the pay period
- **Federal Income Tax:** deduction required by law that supports the federal government
- **FICA (Federal Insurance Contributions Act):** deduction required by law that helps fund Social Security and Medicare
- **State Income Tax:** deduction required by law in most states that supports the state government
- **OASDI (Old-Age, Survivors, and Disability Insurance):** deduction required by law that supports retired people and those who are disabled or their dependents
- **Medicare Tax:** deduction required that provides health insurance for anyone age 65 and older
- **Net Pay:** amount of take-home pay for the pay period after all deductions

Name: ______________________________ Date: ____________________

Assessment

Directions: Fill in the bubble next to the correct answer for each multiple-choice question.

1. Which tax provides for federal health insurance?
   - ❍ A. State income tax
   - ❍ B. Federal income tax
   - ❍ C. Social Security tax
   - ❍ D. Medicare tax

2. Your pay stub lists your pay and deductions for
   - ❍ A. the current pay period.
   - ❍ B. the year-to-date period.
   - ❍ C. the current six months.
   - ❍ D. the current pay period and year-to-date period.

3. Which tax helps support Social Security and Medicare?
   - ❍ A. State income tax
   - ❍ B. Federal income tax
   - ❍ C. FICA
   - ❍ D. OASDI

4. An example of a mandatory withholding is
   - ❍ A. medical insurance.
   - ❍ B. 401(k) plan.
   - ❍ C. Medicare.
   - ❍ D. property tax.

5. Which tax provides disability benefits?
   - ❍ A. State income tax
   - ❍ B. Federal income tax
   - ❍ C. OASDI
   - ❍ D. Medicare tax

6. State income taxes are withheld
   - ❍ A. in all 50 states.
   - ❍ B. in most states.
   - ❍ C. in half the states.
   - ❍ D. in a few states.

Constructed Response

Explain the difference between gross income and net income. How does understanding this difference help you better manage your money? Use details from the reading selection to support your answer. Write the answer in the box.

Name: ______________________ Date: ______________

Knowledge Builder

Paycheck Math

Directions: Review the math examples, then answer the questions.

Paycheck Math

Convert a Percent to a Decimal: Divide the decimal by 100 (*x*/100)

Example: 6% is 6/100 = 0.06 **Example:** 15% is 15/100 = 0.15

Calculate Wages: Kathy earns $7.25 per hour and works 40 hours per week.

Weekly Wage: Multiply the hourly wage by the number of hours worked per week.

Example: $7.25 per hour x 40 hours = $290.00

Gross Yearly Wage: Multiply the total weekly wage by the total number of weeks in a year (52).

Example: $290 wage x 52 weeks = $15,080

1. Terry earns $15.00 an hour as a mechanic. He works 40 hours a week. How much is his weekly gross pay?

2. What is Terry's gross yearly pay?

3. How much is deducted from Terry's gross weekly pay for the following taxes?

   Federal (12%) $ ________

   State (4.95%) $ ________

   Social Security (6.2 %) $ ________

   Medicare (1.45%) $ ________

4. What is Terry's weekly net pay?

Name: ______________________ Date: ______________________

Knowledge Builder

Decoding an Earnings Statement

Directions: Review the earnings statement and then answer the questions.

ABC Super Mart **EARNINGS STATEMENT**

EMPLOYEE NAME	SOCIAL SEC NO.	EMPLOYEE ID	CHECK NO.	PAY PERIOD	PAY DATE
JANE DOE	xxx-xx-2345	202	303	6/8 – 6/19	6/20

INCOME	RATE	HOURS	CURRENT TOTAL
Gross Income	12.25	40.00	490.00

DEDUCTIONS	CURRENT TOTAL	YEAR TO DATE
FEDERAL TAX	49.00	530.00
SOCIAL SECURITY TAX	7.11	78.21
MEDICARE TAX	30.38	334.18
STATE TAX	24.26	266.86

YTD GROSS INCOME	YTD DEDUCTIONS	YTD NET INCOME	CURRENT TOTAL	CURRENT DEDUCTIONS	NET INCOME
5,390.00	1,209.25	4,181.75	490.00	110.75	379.25

ABC Super Mart
202 West Main Street
Madison, NY 13402

Check Number: 303
Pay Date: 6/20/2024

Pay ***Three hundred seventy-nine dollars and 25 cents************************$379.25

To the Order of
Jane Doe
1112 North Hill
Madison, NY 13402

Marcia Adams

1. What was Jane's gross pay for this pay period? ______________
2. What was her net pay? ______________
3. What voluntary deduction payment was taken out of her paycheck? ______________
4. How much does Jane make per hour? ______________
5. Name the mandatory withholding payments from her paycheck, along with their dollar amounts. ______________
6. Why was Jane's net pay less than her gross pay? ______________

Income Tax

Individual, or personal, **income tax** is a tax on the money an individual earns each year. The federal government and most states collect personal income tax. The tax is a percentage of the money someone earns on the job. The more you make, the higher percentage you pay.

The government has set up a system with employers to make the reporting and collecting of federal and state income taxes more convenient for taxpayers. Money that employers withhold from an employee's paycheck is called a withholding tax. This money goes to the government and is credited against their tax bill when they file their income tax returns. Employers withhold money for federal income taxes, Social Security and Medicare taxes, and state and local income taxes.

Tax Responsibilities

The federal agency that collects taxes is the **Internal Revenue Service (IRS)**. The agency in charge of state income tax is the state's **Department of Revenue**. If the taxpayer's total tax payments are greater than the total tax due, they receive a **refund** from the government.

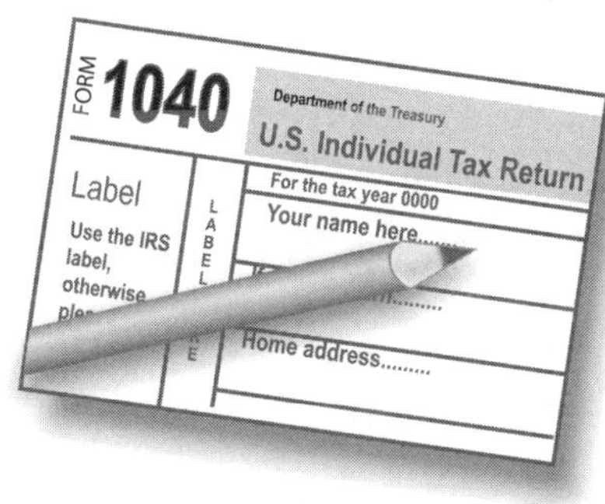

Employers are required to withhold income tax payments from your paychecks. These are based on estimates of how much will be owed at the end of the year. Employers prepare a W-2 form for each employee and send a copy to the employee as well as the IRS and the Social Security Administration. The W-2 form details the employee's annual earnings and the taxes withheld from their paycheck. The taxpayer uses the information to fill out their 1040 form, formally known as the "U.S. Individual Income Tax Return."

United States citizens and permanent residents are required to file a 1040 form based on their **gross income**, or the total amount they earn over the year before deductions such as Social Security and Medicare are taken out. **Net income** is gross income minus all the taxes and other deductions. This is what is known as **take-home pay**.

Taxpayers are responsible for accurately reporting all their income and filing the 1040 form on time. If taxpayers fail to file on time or report incorrect information, they may be subject to penalties.

Filing Tax Returns

The deadline for paying personal income tax is April 15th of each year. Taxpayers are legally responsible for preparing and submitting a tax return to the Internal Revenue Service. Taxpayers may fill out and file their own taxes. There are instructions and computer programs available to provide help in figuring the correct tax to pay. However, many people hire a professional tax preparer to prepare and file their tax returns. People can send their tax returns through the post office, but an increasing number of taxpayers use electronic filing.

Tax evasion, which is trying to avoid paying taxes, is illegal. The IRS may **levy** (seize) assets such as wages and bank accounts plus your personal property, including your car, boat, or home.

Name: ______________________ Date: ______________

Assessment

Directions: Answer the questions in complete sentences. Use information from the reading selection to support your answers.

1. What is the difference between gross income and net income?	2. Explain what happens when the amount of taxes withheld from your earnings is greater than what you owe.
3. What is the purpose of the W-2 form?	4. What are the potential financial risks of avoiding taxes illegally?
5. What is the responsibility of a taxpayer?	6. What is the role of the employer in their employees' income tax withholding?

Name: ______________________ Date: ______________________

Knowledge Builder

Form W-2

American taxpayers receive a W-2 Form each year. Employers prepare the form at the end of the year and submit it to their employees as well as the IRS and the Social Security Administration. It details annual earnings and the taxes withheld from each paycheck. It is important to understand the information reported in this form because you will use this form to file your federal and state taxes.

Directions: Examine the sample W-2 Form below.

25252

a Employee's social security number: xxx-xx-1111

OMB No. 1545-0008 | Safe, accurate, FAST! Use IRS e-file | Visit the IRS website at www.irs.gov/efile.

b Employer identification number (EIN): 25-5XXXXXX

c Employer's name, address, and ZIP code:
Candie Cane Mercantile
123 Main Street
Verona, MO 65769

d Control number

e Employee's first name and initial | Last name | Suff.
Cathy Brownie
2024 Lawrence Street
Verona, MO 65769

f Employee's address and ZIP code

1 Wages, tips, other compensation: 50,000.00	2 Federal income tax withheld: 5,700.00
3 Social security wages: 50,000.00	4 Social security tax withheld: 3,100.00
5 Medicare wages and tips: 50,000.00	6 Medicare tax withheld: 725.00
7 Social security tips	8 Allocated tips
9	10 Dependent care benefits
11 Nonqualified plans	12a See instructions for box 12 (Code)
13 Statutory employee ☐ Retirement plan ☐ Third-party sick pay ☐	12b (Code)
14 Other	12c (Code)
	12d (Code)

15 State	Employer's state ID number	16 State wages, tips, etc.	17 State income tax	18 Local wages, tips, etc.	19 Local income tax	20 Locality name
MO	25-1234567	50,000.00	2,475.00	50,000.00	1,250.00	Verona

Form **W-2** Wage and Tax Statement **2024** Department of the Treasury—Internal Revenue Service

Copy B—To Be Filed With Employee's FEDERAL Tax Return.
This information is being furnished to the Internal Revenue Service.

Three Parts of a W-2 Form

- Left side: reports personal information of the employer and employee
- Right side: reports employee wages, taxes withheld, and benefits
- Bottom: reports employee's state and local tax information

Boxes on W-2 Form

The six boxes labeled A-F contain the personal information of the employer and employee. The twenty numbered boxes contain information to help explain your wages. If a box is left empty, that means the information does not pertain to your wages or taxes.

Name: ______________________ Date: ______________________

Knowledge Builder (cont.)

Form 1040

Directions: Use the information from the Form W-2 on page 47 to complete this simplified version of a Form 1040. For this example, Cathy Brownie is single with no dependents and cannot be claimed as a dependent by anyone else. Line 7 has been filled in for you.

Form 1040 — Income Tax Return for Single Filers With No Dependents

Name and Address

Name (first, initial, last)

Home address

City, State, Zip Code

Your social security number ___ ___ ___ - ___ ___ - ___ ___ ___ ___

Report your income

1. Total wages, salaries, and tips. See your W-2 form. ___ ___, ___ ___ ___. ___ ___
2. Taxable interest income of $1,500 or less. ___ ___ ___. ___ ___
3. Add lines 1 and 2. This is your **adjusted gross income.** ___ ___, ___ ___ ___. ___ ___
4. Can your parents (or someone else) claim you on their return?
   ____ Yes. See tax pamphlet for information.
   _X_ No. Enter 13,850.00. This is the total of your standard deduction and personal exemption. ___ ___, ___ ___ ___. ___ ___
5. Subtract line 4 from line 3. If line 4 is larger than line 3, enter 0. This is your **taxable income.** ___ ___, ___ ___ ___. ___ ___

Figure your tax

6. Enter your Federal income tax withheld on your W-2 form(s). ___ ___, ___ ___ ___. ___ ___
7. **Tax.** Look at line 5 above. Use the amount on **line 5** to find your tax in the tax table in the tax return pamphlet. Then enter the tax from the table on this line. 4,121.00

Refund or amount you owe

8. If line 6 is larger than line 7, subtract line 7 from line 6. This is your **refund.** ___, ___ ___ ___. ___ ___
9. If line 7 is larger than line 6, subtract line 6 from line 7. This is the **amount you owe.** Attach your payment for full amount payable to the "Internal Revenue Service." Write your name, address, social security number, daytime phone number, and "Tax Form 1040" on it. ___, ___ ___ ___. ___ ___

Sign your return

I have read this return. I declare that it is true, correct, and complete to the best of my knowledge.

Your signature X ______________________ Date ______________________

Checking

A **checking account** is a type of bank account that allows you to put money in and take money out to pay for daily expenses. Getting money in or out of the account is called a **transaction**. Putting money in is called a **deposit**, and taking money out is called a **withdrawal**. There are several types of transactions, including:

- **Cash** – Money you can deposit or withdraw from your account at the bank.
- **Check** – A piece of paper that instructs a bank to pay a specific amount to the **bearer**, the person or business to whom the check is written. The bank charges a penalty fee for **overdrafts**. This occurs when you do not have enough money in your account to cover the transaction.
- **Debit Card** – A plastic card issued by your bank. It works as an ATM card and credit card, but the money comes directly out of your checking account electronically.
- **Online Banking** – You can make transactions using a computer or mobile device.

Checkbook

When you open a checking account with a bank, you will receive a **checkbook** to help you keep track of your transactions. The checkbook contains checks, deposit slips, and the checkbook register.

Parts of a Check

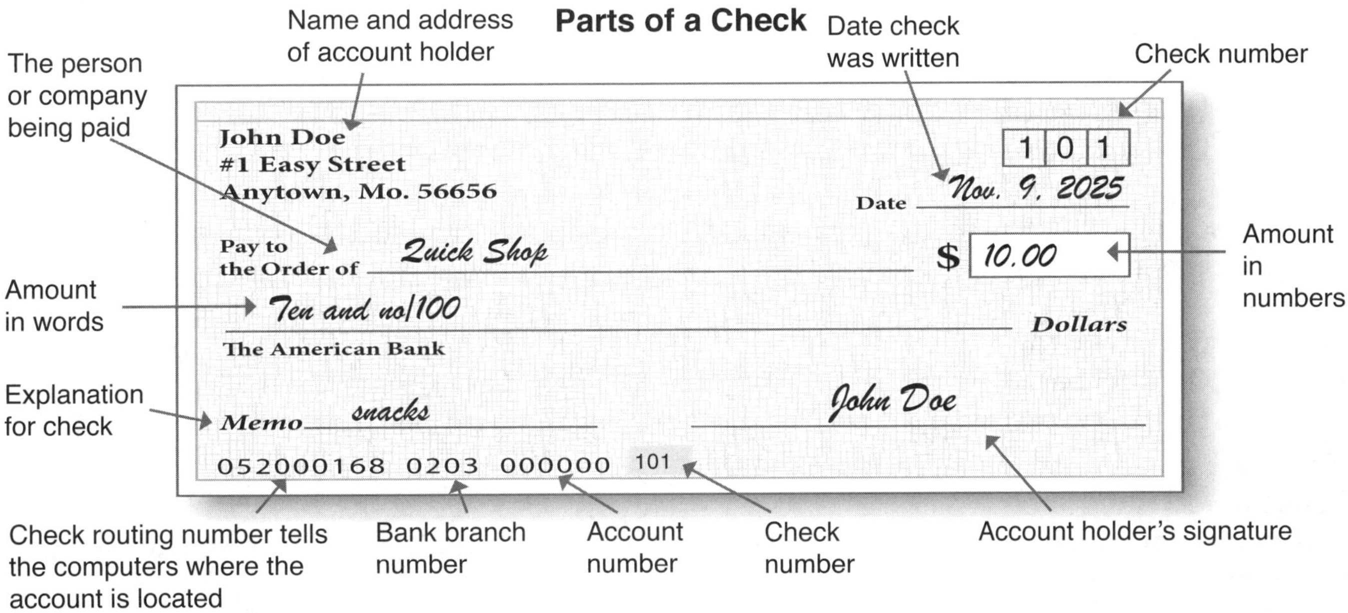

Checkbook Register

A **register** is a record of all deposits and withdrawals from a checking account. You can also use a checkbook app to keep track of transactions. Deposits are added to the account. Check, debit card, or online withdrawals are subtracted.

Check Number	*Date*	*Description of Transaction*	*Payment*	*Deposit*	*Balance*
					$450.00
101	11/9	Quick Shop	$10.00		– 10.00
					440.00
	11/30	Deposit		$429.00	+ 429.00
					869.00

Name: ______________________ Date: ______________________

Assessment

Directions: Complete the page using information from the reading selection.

Fill in the Blanks

1. A checking account is used for day-to-day ______________ like writing checks and bill payments.
2. A ______________ is a record of all deposits and withdrawals from a checking account.
3. ______________ ______________ allows you to make transactions using a mobile device.
4. An ______________ occurs when you don't have enough money in your account to cover a transaction.

Multiple Choice

5. Money taken out of your checking account
   - ❍ A. deposit
   - ❍ B. overdraft
   - ❍ C. withdrawal
   - ❍ D. endorsement

6. A plastic card issued by your bank that works as an ATM and credit card
   - ❍ A. deposit card
   - ❍ B. bank card
   - ❍ C. debit card
   - ❍ D. checking account card

7. A piece of paper that instructs a bank to pay a specific amount to the bearer
   - ❍ A. check
   - ❍ B. overdraft
   - ❍ C. deposit
   - ❍ D. endorsement

8. Transactions using a computer or mobile device
   - ❍ A. online banking
   - ❍ B. cell phone banking
   - ❍ C. computer banking
   - ❍ D. easy banking

Constructed Response

What are the advantages to having an individual checking account? Use details from the reading selection to support your answer. Write the answer in the box.

Name: ______________________ Date: ______________________

Knowledge Builder

A Deposit Slip

A **deposit slip** is used to add funds to a bank account. Funds can be checks or cash. When depositing a check in your account, you are required to write your signature on the back. The signature on the back of the check is called an **endorsement**. It authorizes the bank to process the check.

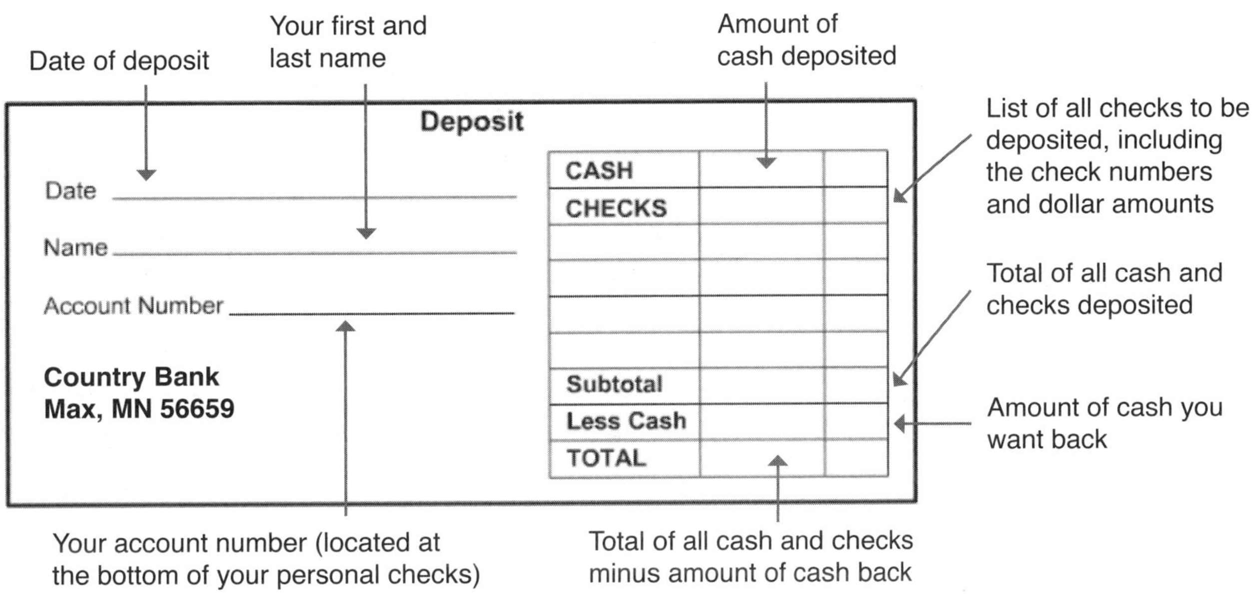

Directions: Complete the deposit slip using today's date and your name. Your account number is 1234567. You are depositing the following items into your checking account.

1. You received $15.00 in cash from your grandparents as a birthday gift.
2. You received a paycheck (#7439) for $103.00.
3. You received a $20 check (#202) from your neighbor for yardwork.

Deposit

Date ______________________

Name ______________________

Account Number ______________________

Country Bank
Max, MN 56659

CASH		
CHECKS		
Subtotal		
Less Cash		
TOTAL		

Name: ______________________ Date: ______________________

Knowledge Builder

Check Writing

Steps for Writing a Check

1. Write the date.
2. Name the recipient.
3. Fill in the amount with numerals.
4. Write out the amount in words. Use a fraction for the cents.
5. Write the purpose for the check in the memo.
6. Sign your name.

John Doe
#1 Easy Street
Anytown, MO 56656

102

Date *July 15, 2025*

Pay to the Order of *Pizza Palace* $ *24.95*

Twenty-four and 95/100 ------------------ Dollars

North Main Bank
200 N. Main St.
Anytown, MO 56656

Memo *lunch* *John Doe*

052000168 0203 000000 102

Directions: Fill in the blanks on the check below. Your phone bill of $89.24 to the PhoneTel Company is due October 19, 2025. Write a check to the company.

213

Name: ______________________
Address: ______________________
____

Date ______________________

Pay to the Order of ______________________ $ ________

______________________ Dollars

Great Mountain Bank
72 Slope Drive
Cascade, CO 80809

Memo ______________________ ______________________

062100598 1122 1234578 213

Directions: Add the PhoneTel check to the register below. Calculate your new balance.

Check Number	Date	Description of Transaction	Payment	Deposit	Balance $450.00
212	8/21	Half Price Store	$25.08		– 25.08
					424.92

Debit Cards

A **debit card** is a plastic card issued by your bank. The card allows you to spend money you already have in your bank checking account. When you use the card, the money comes directly out of your account electronically. Online banking and the use of a mobile banking app are ways to track debit card transactions. Some people choose to save debit card information to a digital wallet. A **digital wallet** is an app that stores your debit card payment information and allows you to make electronic transactions using devices such as your cell phone, smartwatch, laptop, tablet, and computer. The transaction information is electronically transferred to your bank.

Using a Debit Card

Debit cards make shopping convenient. The cards are accepted by most businesses, so you don't need to carry cash or a checkbook. You can use them to make purchases online, pay bills, and withdraw cash from an ATM. Some banks will allow you to deposit cash at an ATM that takes cash deposits.

A debit card can help you manage your spending. Your mobile banking app allows you to check your account balance before making a purchase with your debit card. Banks allow you to set daily limits on debit cards to help prevent overspending.

Debit cards are a secure way to shop. They offer security features like chip technology and PINs to protect your account. A **Personal Identification Number (PIN)** is a number code that verifies your identity when making a purchase. Debit card issuers also offer 24-hour fraud monitoring services. This allows you to remotely turn off your card to prevent unauthorized use if your card is lost or stolen.

Debit cards don't incur interest charges because your debit card instantly deducts money from your checking account. Because you aren't borrowing from a lender as with a credit card, you are not charged interest each month.

There are usually no fees for debit card use. If there are charges, they are often related to the bank's monthly maintenance fees. Some banks will charge a small fee for using ATMs other than their own.

Tracking Debit Spending

There are several ways to check your debit card spending:

- Write down your debit card transactions, including ATM withdrawals.
- Keep all your receipts so you can check what transactions you have made.
- Use your bank's app to check your bank statement for account balance and transactions as often as you need.
- Check your balance at an ATM.
- Call your bank's customer service or visit a bank branch and speak with a teller.
- Ask your bank to send you email or text alerts when your balance goes below a certain amount.

Debit Card Information

It is important to protect your debit card information. Don't share your card number, expiration date, or security code with anyone you don't trust. Report lost or stolen cards immediately.

Name: ______________________________ Date: ______________________

Assessment

Directions: Fill in the bubble next to the correct answer for each multiple-choice question.

1. When you use a debit card to make a purchase, the money comes from your
   ❍ A. ATM account.
   ❍ B. savings account.
   ❍ C. checking account.
   ❍ D. credit account.

2. Your mobile banking app
   ❍ A. offers 1 year fraud monitoring services.
   ❍ B. charges interest.
   ❍ C. allows you to check your account balance.
   ❍ D. charges monthly maintenance fees.

3. Which of the following people should know your PIN?
   ❍ A. only you
   ❍ B. your siblings
   ❍ C. your best friend
   ❍ D. your parents

4. When do you typically receive a debit card?
   ❍ A. when you turn 16 years old
   ❍ B. when you open a checking account
   ❍ C. when you start a new job
   ❍ D. when you begin paying taxes

5. Debit cards don't incur interest charges because
   ❍ A. money is deducted from your checking account.
   ❍ B. there are limited fees for debit card use.
   ❍ C. a debit card is a bank loan.
   ❍ D. interest is only charged for ATM transactions.

6. What do you receive at the end of a billing cycle to detail all of your monthly debit card transactions?
   ❍ A savings invoice
   ❍ B. bank statement
   ❍ C. overdraft notice
   ❍ D. interest notification

Constructed Response

What is a digital wallet? Use details from the reading selection to support your answer. Write your answer in the box.

Name: ______________________________ Date: ____________________

Knowledge Builder

Parts of a Debit Card

Directions: Review the parts of a debit card. Use the information to answer the questions below.

Understanding Your Debit Card

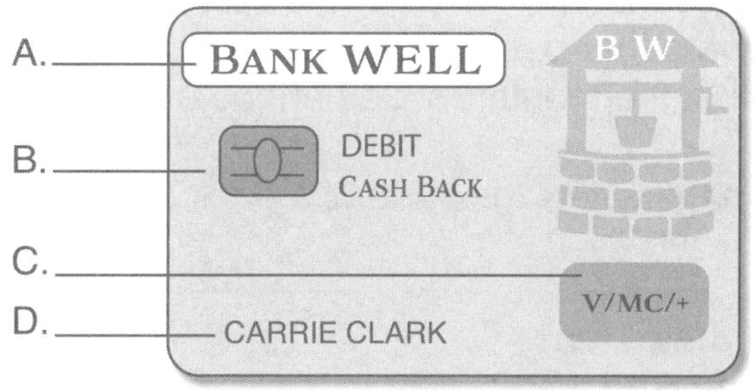

A. **Bank Name:** bank that issued card
B. **Smart Chip (EMV):** security feature; generates a unique code, called a cryptogram, for each transaction
C. **Payment Network Logo** such as Visa® or MasterCard® Logo: symbol means that card can be used wherever that brand of debit cards are accepted
D. **Cardholder's Name**
E. **Magnetic Strip:** security feature; stores account details
F. **Signature Bar:** where cardholder signs their name
G. **Hologram:** security feature; helps prevent fraud and counterfeiting
H. **Account Number:** a 16-digit number unique to the card
I. **Customer Service Number/Website:** call or visit website when customer has questions about their account
J. **Security Code (CVV):** a number unique to the card
K. **Expiration Date:** card's expiration date
L. **Contactless cards** with **near field contact (NFC)** technology allow the customer to pay by tapping the card on or near the payment device.
M. **Payment Network Logo**

Note: Features and locations may vary on individual cards.

Questions

1. What is the name of the bank that issued the debit card? ____________________
2. What is the name of the cardholder? ____________________
3. Where can the card be used? ____________________
4. What should a cardholder do if they have questions about their debit card? ____________________
5. What is the expiration date of this card? ____________________
6. What is this card's account number? ____________________
7. What is the purpose of the card hologram? ____________________

Name: ______________________________ Date: ____________________

Knowledge Builder

Debit Card Bank Statement

A bank statement is a record of all the money going into and out of your bank account. Deposits and credits are money going into your account. A withdrawal or debit is money going out of your account. The layout of the bank statement varies from bank to bank, but all statements contain the same basic information. Your statement is available on your bank app, or you can request that the monthly statement be emailed or sent to your mailing address.

Directions: Review the parts of a bank statement. Use the information to answer the questions below.

Middle State Bank
411 North Street
My Town, MI 55555

Account #0012300123004567
Sue Tompson
600 Main Street
My Town, MI 55555

Statement Covers: March 27, 2025 through April 25, 2025

Summary

Beginning Balance	$968.10
Total Deposits	$687.83
Total Withdrawals	$92.90
Fees	$2.00
Ending Balance	$1,561.03

Deposits & Credits

Date	Transaction	Amount
03/30	Deposit at Middle State Bank	$587.83
04/20	Deposit at Middle State Bank	$100.00

Withdrawals

Date	Transaction	Amount
04/11 Debit Card	T-shirt Palace	$42.90
04/15 ATM	Cash	$50.00
04/15 ATM Fee	Bank Fee	$2.00

1. What is the name and address of the bank? ____________________
2. Who is the owner of the account? ____________________
3. What is the account number? ____________________
4. Why was the account charged a fee? ____________________
5. Where was the debit card used to make a purchase? ____________________
6. Explain why the account's ending balance is more than the beginning balance. ____________________

____

Savings

There are many reasons you might want to save your money. You can build up your savings to buy something big like a cell phone or to use for a school field trip.

Once you have saved some money, you will want to find a place to keep it. A bank is a safe place to keep your money. **The Federal Deposit Insurance Corporation (FDIC)** insures checking and savings accounts for up to $250,000. This means the insurance will pay back the money in your account if it is lost or the bank closes. A seal on the door of the bank will tell you if it is covered by the FDIC.

Savings Account

Savings accounts allow depositors to store their money at a bank. In return, the bank will pay the depositor **interest**, a fee for allowing the bank to use the depositor's money. The bank uses the money to make loans to other customers. The customers pay the bank interest on the loans. Part of the interest goes to the depositor and part to the bank. Interest from loans is how the bank makes money.

Questions to Ask

There are many banks to choose from, including full-service banks, credit unions, or savings and loan banks. They all handle savings accounts. Research banks in your area until you find one that meets your needs. There are several questions to ask a bank before opening an account:

1. Is a minimum amount of money needed to open an account? Some banks require a minimum deposit to open a savings account. The amount can vary from $5 to $100 or more.
2. Does the bank charge a fee for holding the account? Many banks charge fees to maintain a savings account. Fees can be one-time or ongoing. These fees are often called monthly service fees or maintenance fees, and they can range from $4 to $25 per month.
3. How much interest does the bank pay? Most savings accounts earn interest, but the rate can vary. Banks pay interest as a percentage of your balance to encourage you to keep your money with them.
4. Can you withdraw your money at any time? Generally, you can withdraw money from a savings account at any time, but some banks may limit how often you can withdraw cash. For example, some banks limit the number of withdrawals or transfers to six per month and charge a fee for each withdrawal over that limit. The cost may be as much as $10 per transaction.
5. Is the bank conveniently located so you can easily make regular deposits? If you have a financial emergency, you do not want to travel a long distance to get cash.

Name: ______________________ Date: ______________

Assessment

Directions: Write *T* if the statement is true. Write *F* if the statement is false. If the statement is false, rewrite the answer below the statement to make it true.

_____ 1. Banks do not require a minimum deposit to open a savings account.

_____ 2. There are fees associated with a savings account.

_____ 3. A savings account is designed to hold money that is not needed for daily expenses.

_____ 4. Savings accounts don't usually pay interest on the money you deposit.

_____ 5. A bank uses a depositor's money to make loans to other customers.

_____ 6. A savings account allows you to deposit and withdraw money.

_____ 7. The FDIC is a bank that offers high interest rates for saving accounts.

Constructed Response

What are the advantages to having a savings account? Use details from the reading selection to support your answer. Write the answer in the box.

Name: ______________________________ Date: ____________________

Knowledge Builder

Interest

A savings account is a safe place to store and grow your money. Your money is insured by the Federal Deposit Insurance Corporation, and banks will pay you interest, a fee, to keep your money in the account. Depending on the bank, the interest may be calculated and added to your account daily, monthly, or yearly.

Suppose you deposit $1,000 into a savings account, don't deposit or withdraw any more money, and the interest rate doesn't change. If the account has a 1% annual interest rate and the bank pays you interest on your balance once each year, you will earn $10 after the first year.

How to Calculate Interest

To calculate interest, multiply the starting balance by the interest rate and the length of time the money has been on deposit.

Formula for calculating interest: $P \times R \times T = I$

- P — principal (the amount deposited into savings)
- R — rate of interest (written as decimals)
- T — time (the length of time the money has been deposited)
- I — interest earned

Example: You deposit $100 into your savings account. You do not deposit or withdraw any money over a two-year period. How much interest will you earn in 1 year at an interest rate of 4% per year?

$100 (principal) x 0.04 (interest) x 1 year = 04.00 or $4.00

After 1 year, you'll have earned $4.00 in interest. This is added to your savings account. So, your new savings account balance will be $104.00. Each year, the interest is calculated on the previous year's balance.

Time	Interest Earned	New Balance
1 year	$4.00	$104.00
2 years	$4.16	$108.16

Directions: Complete the table. You deposit $100 into your new savings account. The annual interest rate is 5%. You do not deposit or withdraw any money over a four-year period.

Time	Interest Earned	New Balance
1 year		
2 years		
3 years		
4 years		

Name: ______________________ Date: ______________

Knowledge Builder

Choosing a Bank

Directions: Research three banks in your area. Use the information to complete the checklist below.

Bank Checklist			
Information	**Bank #1 Name**	**Bank #2 Name**	**Bank #3 Name**
1. Is my money insured by the FDIC?			
2. What is the interest rate for a savings account?			
3. How much money do I need to open an account?			
4. How much do I need to keep in my account to avoid fees?			
5. Does this account have a maturity date? (a date the bank stops paying interest or that you can withdraw money without losing some interest)			
6. Can I withdraw my savings when I need it?			
7. How many withdrawals can I make each month?			
8. Is the bank conveniently located?			

9. Which bank would be the best place for you to start a savings account?

____

Loans

Borrowing money is a way to purchase something now and pay for it over time. People often borrow money or get a loan for big-ticket items such as a car or home. Borrowing money will ultimately cost you more than paying for the item at the time of purchase.

A Loan

Banks, credit unions, and online lenders are common sources of funds for people wanting a loan. A **loan** is a contract between a borrower and a lender. The borrower promises to pay the lender back all the money in a certain amount of time. The borrower must also pay the lender **interest**, or a fee to get the loan.

Three Parts of a Loan

Loans are usually term loans. This means the person borrowing the money is required to pay the money back over a certain period of time, usually in months. The length of the loan varies depending on the type of loan and the lending institution. Some lenders offer one-year or less loans, while others offer repayment periods of 10 years or longer. The shorter the term, the higher the payment. The longer the term, the smaller the payments will be.

The loan **principal** is the amount borrowed. It is the amount you will need to pay back over the loan's length. The **interest rate** is the fee charged for borrowing the money, shown as a percentage of the principal. Each month, you make a payment on your loan. Some money goes to pay the principal and some for interest.

Loan Payment Schedule

Lenders provide the borrower with a repayment schedule. This lets the borrower know when to start paying on the loan, how often they make payments, and the minimum, or lowest, payment amount required. Most loan payments are required each month. It is important to make the payments on time. Not paying on time could lead to the borrower being fined, taken to court, or placed in jail.

As the loan is paid off, the balance decreases, and more of the payment goes toward the principal and less toward interest. Lenders use a payment calculator to determine what your monthly payment will be.

Example: A loan for $10,000.00 at a rate of 10% interest over 4 years

Principal x Interest Rate x Time (years) = Total Interest

$10,000.00 x 0.1 x 4 = $4,000.00

Total Interest ÷ # of Months in Loan = Monthly Interest

$4,000,00 ÷ 48 = $83.33

The lender's payment calculator has determined the monthly payment will be $253.63. Each month, the following formula determines how much goes toward the principal and how much goes toward the interest so that the loan will be paid off by the end of the four years.

Payment – Interest = Principal

Beginning Balance – Principal = Ending Balance

Loan Payment Schedule (first two months)					
Months	**Beginning Balance**	**Payment**	**Interest**	**Principal**	**Ending Balance**
1	$10,000.00	$253.63	$83.33	$170.30	$9,829.70
2	$9,829.70	$253.63	$81.91	$171.72	$9,657.98

Name: ______________________________ Date: ______________________

Assessment

Directions: Use information from the reading selection to answer the questions. Write your answers in complete sentences.

1. What is a loan?	
2. What is an interest rate?	
3. Why is a loan payment schedule important?	
4. What is a term loan?	
5. What are the penalties for not repaying a loan?	

Directions: Complete the Loan Payment Schedule for a $7,000 loan at 5% interest over 4 years.

Loan Payment Schedule (first four months)					
Months	**Beginning Balance**	**Payment**	**Interest**	**Principal**	**Ending Balance**
1	$7,000.00	$209.80	$29.17		$6,819.37
2	$6,819.37		$28.41	$181.39	$6,637.98
3		$209.80	$27.66	$182.14	$6,455.84
4	$6,455.84	$209.80	$26.90	$182.90	

Name: ______________________________ Date: ______________________

Knowledge Builder

Calculating a Car Loan Payment

Directions: Follow the examples to complete the down payment table.

You decide to buy a used car. Used car loans typically require a down payment. A **down payment** is the money paid upfront toward a vehicle purchase. A down payment is usually around 10% of the car's total cost. To find the loan amount, subtract the down payment from the purchase price of the car.

Example: Down payment for a $15,000 car
$15,000 (purchase price) x 10% (0.1) = $1,500 (down payment)

Example: Loan total after down payment for a $15,000 car
$15,000 (purchase price) – $1,500 (down payment) = $13,500 (loan amount)

	Car #1	Car #2	Car #3
Car Price	$12,000	$17,000	$25,000
10% Down Payment			
Amount of Bank Loan			

Directions: Follow the example to complete the monthly payment table for three different car loans. (This table does not include interest.)

Most car loans are from 36 months (3 years) to 60 months (5 years). The shorter the term, the higher the payment. The longer the term, the smaller the payments will be.

Example: Loan Amount ÷ Number of Months = Monthly Payment
$10,000 (amount) ÷ 36 (months) = $277.78 monthly payment
Remember: round the payment amount to the nearest hundredth

	Car #1	Car #2	Car #3
Amount of Bank Loan	$11,000	$18,000	$20,000
Number of Months	36	48	60
Monthly Payment			

Name: ______________________ Date: ______________

Knowledge Builder

Buying a Car

Directions: You are ready to buy your first vehicle. You decide to buy a used car. Research three cars you think you might be interested in purchasing. Write the car's make, model, year, and purchase price in the table. Follow the formulas below, and complete the table.

Example:

Purchase Price x % of Tax (7%) = Tax
Purchase Price – Down Payment (10%) + Tax = Loan Amount
Loan Amount x Interest Rate x Number of Years = Interest
Loan Amount + Interest = Total Loan Amount
Total Loan Amount ÷ Number of Months of the Loan = Monthly Car Payment

Calculating Loan Amount and Monthly Car Payment			
	Car #1	**Car #2**	**Car #3**
Make (company that makes the car)			
Model (the specific name of the car) & Year			
Purchase Price			
Down Payment 10% (0.1)			
Sales Tax 7% (0.07)			
Loan Amount			
Loan Term	5 years	5 years	5 years
Interest Rate	10% (0.1)	10% (0.1)	10% (0.1)
Interest			
Total Loan Amount			
Number of Months			
Monthly Car Payment			

Which car would be the best buy for you? Why? ______________________

____

Credit Cards

A **credit card** is a plastic card issued by businesses such as banks, credit unions, and retail stores to customers they trust. When someone uses a credit card, no money changes hands. The purchaser charges the amount to their card, takes the goods home, and is billed monthly until the amount of the purchase is paid. A charge to a credit card is considered a loan, and the cardholder is charged **interest** (a fee) for borrowing the money.

A credit card lets you spend up to an agreed amount, which is called your **credit limit**. The exact amount will depend on your credit history and income. A **credit history** is a record of how you handle money and **debt**, or money you owe. **Credit bureaus** are companies that collect this type of information. The information is used to determine your **credit rating or score**. This three-digit number represents whether or not you are a person who can be trusted to borrow money. A good credit score is considered anywhere from 690 to 850, with 850 being an excellent credit score.

Parts of a Credit Card

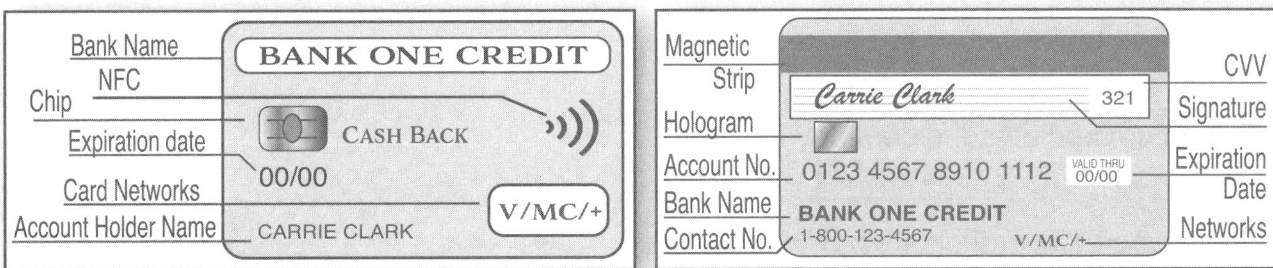

The chip, CVV code, and hologram are security features that help prevent fraud and counterfeiting. The magnetic strip contains information about the card.

Using a Credit Card

When a customer uses a credit card, the business that issued the card pays for the customer's purchases. The business sends the customer a monthly **billing statement** that lists purchases, payments, interest charges, card fees, and the account balance. The customer can either pay back the card issuer in full or pay only a portion back and be charged interest on the remaining balance.

Businesses like to issue credit cards since many consumers do not pay their bills in full every month and end up paying high amounts of interest to the company. The interest rate can vary based on a customer's credit and payment history. Businesses reserve the right to deny credit to any customer they feel is a bad risk or might not be able to repay the debt.

Credit cards can be used in three ways: physically at a store, over the phone, or on the internet.

- **Charging at store or business:** The card is swiped through a credit card reader at the register. The reader scans the magnetic strip on the back of the card, which contains information about the card. The card may also contain a chip and be inserted in a chip reader instead of being swiped. The reader then confirms the information and authorizes the purchase.
- **Charging over the phone or internet:** The cardholder provides a business with information such as the credit card number, expiration date, full name on the card, the cardholder's address, and CVV code.

Name: ______________________________ Date: ____________________

Assessment

Directions: Complete the page using information from the reading selections.

Matching

_____ 1. credit card
_____ 2. debts
_____ 3. credit score
_____ 4. billing statement

A. record of purchases, payments, interest charges, card fees, and the account balance
B. used to determine whether or not a person is a good credit risk
C. money owed
D. method of buying on credit with payments over an extended period of time

Question/Answer

5. What is interest? ______________________________
____
6. When do credit cardholders pay interest? ______________________________
____
7. Why do credit cardholders pay interest? ______________________________
____
8. What is the purpose of the chip, CVV code, and hologram that appear on a credit card?
____
____

Constructed Response

Explain the advantages and disadvantages to using a credit card. Use details from the reading selection to support your answer. Write your answer in the box.

Name: ______________________________ Date: ____________________

Knowledge Builder

Credit Card Statement

Directions: Review Michael's credit card statement. Use the information to answer the questions below.

Account Statement

Summary of Account Activity

Previous Balance	$4,001.91
Payments	-$1,000.00
Purchases	+$1,317.44
Cash Advances	+$0.00
Fees Charged	+$0.00
Interest Charged	+$72.96
New Balance	$4,392.31
Past Due	$0.00

Account Summary

Credit Limit	$13,700.00
Available Credit	$9,307.00
Cash Advance Limit	$250.00
Available Cash Limit	$250.00
Amount Over Credit Limit	$0.00
Statement Closing Date	04/26/2025
Next Statement Closing Date	05/28/2025
Days in Billing Cycle	29

Payment Information

New Balance	$4,392.31
Minimum Payment Due	$117.00
Payment Due Date	May 24, 2025

Late Payment Warning: If we do not receive your minimum payment by the payment due date, you may have to pay a late fee of up to $40.

Minimum Payment Warning: If you make only the minimum payment each period, you will pay more interest, and it will take you longer to pay off the balance.

Date of Transaction	Transaction Description	Amount
04/10/2025	Payment - thank you	$1,000.00
04/15/2025	Last Stop Auto Repair	$910.36
04/22/2025	Buy Right Electronics	$407.08

Questions

1. What is Michael's current credit card balance? ____________
2. What is the total amount Michael charged to the credit card this billing cycle? ____________
3. How much was the latest card payment? ____________
4. What is the minimum payment Michael must make? ____________
5. How much is the credit limit for the card? ____________
6. How much interest will be charged this month? ____________
7. When is the payment due? ____________
8. What will happen if Michael only makes minimum payments each billing cycle? ____________

____

Name: ________________________ Date: ________________

Knowledge Builder

Credit Card Application

Directions: Review the information in the credit card application scenario. Use your personal information and the information from the scenario to complete the application.

Scenario: You are applying for a credit card. You have worked at Pet Fun as a cashier for 2 years. The store is located at 9981 Main Street in Monette, Arkansas. The zip code is 72447. The store phone number is 417-555-0144. You work 40 hours a week and make $17.00 an hour. You have a checking and savings account at Hometown Bank in Monette, Arkansas. Your checking account number is 0012345678, and your savings account number is 0087654321.

Credit Card Application				
Name (Last, First, Middle)		Street Address		
City	State	Zip Code	Years at address	__ Rent __ Own __ Live w/Parents
Date of Birth	Mother's Maiden Name	Home Phone and Area Code		Are you a U.S. resident? ___ Yes ___ No
Previous Address	City	State	Zip Code	Years there
Employment Information				
Employer		Position		
Work Address	City	State	Zip Code	
Work Phone and Area Code	Social Security Number XXX-XX-XXXX	Years at this employer		
Income Information				
Your yearly income from all sources must be at least $8,000 to be considered for credit card acceptance.		Your total personal yearly income $		
Other household yearly income $		Other yearly income sources $		
Account Information				
Checking Account Institution Name		Account Number		
Savings Account Institution Name		Account Number		
By signing, I authorize The American Bank to check my credit history. I attest that the above information is true. I have read and understand the terms of credit.		Applicant's Signature X	Date	

Investment

Investing is a way to have your money earn money. An **investor** is a person spending money in the hopes of making more. Often, investments involve a certain amount of risk. **Risk** means the investor could end up with less money in the future than invested. Some investments involve no risk, while others involve the possibility of an investor losing some or all of their initial investment. Usually, the more risk involved, the more money the investor could make.

Type of Investments	Description	Risk Factor (RF)
Savings Account	The investor deposits money in a safe place (bank, credit union, or savings and loan association) while earning interest. Interest is a fee paid to the investor, so the money can be used to fund loans.	Banks insure deposits through the Federal Deposit Insurance Corporation (FDIC). This means if an FDIC-insured bank fails, depositors will get up to the $250,000 limit of their deposits back. **(RF: None)**
Certificate of Deposit (CD)	The investor earns a higher rate of interest by depositing money in an account at a bank or credit union. CDs have a maturity date, when the investor can cash in a CD without a penalty or fee.	The Federal Deposit Insurance Corporation (FDIC) protects Certificates of Deposits purchased through a bank. **(RF: None)**
Government Bonds, Corporate Bonds, and Municipal Bonds	The purchaser of a bond is really loaning money to the bond issuer. Upon the bond's maturity, the investor receives a fixed amount of interest along with the initial investment. Bonds usually pay higher interest rates than checking and savings accounts.	The federal government backs government bonds. They pay a fixed amount of interest. **(RF: None)** Corporate and municipal bonds are riskier because of possible default by bond issuers and changing interest rates. **(RF: Low Risk)**
Stocks	The investor buys shares of ownership in a company, anticipating that the stock will increase in value. There is always the risk the stock will decrease in value.	If the company isn't successful, stocks will be worth less than the original purchase price. Selling will result in a capital loss instead of a capital gain. **(RF: High Risk)**
Mutual Funds	The investor becomes a member of a group of investors, which has a professional fund manager who purchases and sells stocks and bonds on behalf of the group.	Mutual funds are vulnerable to the same risk factors as stocks and bonds. Also, the fund manager may not invest the funds wisely. **(RF: High Risk)**

If an investment is sold for more than you bought it, you may be charged a tax by the government. ***Capital gains*** *can apply to almost any investment sold at a profit, such as stocks, bonds, and mutual funds.*

Name: ______________________________ Date: ____________________

Assessment

Directions: Complete the page using information from the reading selection.

Matching

_____ 1. investing

_____ 2. maturity date

_____ 3. penalty

_____ 4. interest

_____ 5. FDIC

A. insurance company that protects bank deposits

B. the date when the investor can cash in a CD without a penalty

C. fee paid to the investor so the money can be used to fund loans

D. fee charged to an investor

E. setting aside income for future use that makes money

Multiple Choice

6. Which would be considered a high-risk investment?
   - ❍ A. stocks
   - ❍ B. savings
   - ❍ C. government bond
   - ❍ D. certificate of deposit

7. A mutual fund account allows investors to
   - ❍ A. pool their money with other investors to buy investments like stocks and bonds.
   - ❍ B. deposit money in a safe place while earning interest.
   - ❍ C. earn interest on their savings.
   - ❍ D. receive a fixed amount of interest.

8. If you buy shares of a company's stock
   - ❍ A. you have lent money to the company.
   - ❍ B. your investment is insured through the FDIC.
   - ❍ C. you own a part of the company.
   - ❍ D. your investment is used to fund loans.

9. What is a capital gains tax?
   - ❍ A. a fee charged for a savings account
   - ❍ B. a fee paid to the investor
   - ❍ C. a fee charged to a professional funds manager
   - ❍ D. a fee charged on any profit made from the sale of bonds and stocks

Constructed Response

Explain why investing in stocks is riskier than a savings account. Use details from the reading selection to support your answer. Write your answer in the box.

Name: ______________________________ Date: ____________________

Knowledge Builder

Reading a Stock Table

Directions: Read the information and answer the following questions.

The **stock market** is a place where people can buy, sell, or trade **stocks**, or shares of companies. A company sells shares to raise money for expansion or research for product development. People who buy stocks are investing in the company. They become **stockholders**, or part owners in the company. If the company grows and makes a profit, the investor can make money. The company may share the profits with the stockholder by paying a **dividend**. The stockholder can also make money by selling the stock when the price per share increases.

Stocks are traded on a variety of stock exchanges throughout the world. One of the largest and most familiar exchanges is the **New York Stock Exchange (NYSE)**. One of the most popular ways to keep track of the up and down movement of the entire stock market is to check the **Dow Jones Industrial Average (DOW)**.

A **stock table** lists information about a company's price changes, current trading price, historical highs and lows, dividends, trading volume, and other company financial information.

Column: 1		2	3	4	5	6
52 Week		Stock, Symbol (SYM), or Name	Split (s)	Year to Date (YTD)	Close or Last	Change (Chg)
High	Low					
14.00	4.15	ARZ		-47.70	4.71	+0.20
39.29	8.70	AAL		-61.70	12.49	+0.17
42.88	28.92	Bk Tw		+10.00	33.10	-0.40
53.75	18.50	BBB	s	+12.90	46.64	-0.84
59.99	36.33	KAT		+28.80	49.25	+0.35
7.10	3.25	CTM		+2.10	6.09	-0.34

Column 1: reports the stock's high and low selling price over the past year

Column 2: reports the stock's name, an abbreviated version of the stock's name, or the stock's symbol used on the exchange

Column 3: reports a stock split. The stocks have been divided into a larger number of lower-priced shares. Example: If a $10.00 share is split 2 for 1, the stockholder ends up with two shares, each worth $5.00.

Column 4: reports % of change in the stock's price either up (+) or down (-) over a year

Column 5: reports the price the stock was selling for at the end of that trading day

Column 6: reports the change in a stock's price, either up (+) or down (-) on that trading day

1. Why is KAT a good choice for investment? ______________________________

____

____

2. Why is AAL not a good choice for investment? ______________________________

____

____

Name: ______________________________ Date: ____________________

Knowledge Builder

Buying and Selling Stocks

Directions: Follow each step to complete the Tracking Table. You will need two copies of the table for the activity.

Week One Steps:

1. You are investing $10,000 in stocks. You are investing $2,000 in each stock. List the amount on the chart.
2. Choose five companies in which to invest. Think about which brands of soda, electronics, clothing, and breakfast cereal or snacks you use or eat.
3. Using the financial page of a major newspaper or the Internet, locate each company's stock details. Use the information to complete the Tracking Table.
4. Calculate the number of shares you were able to purchase for each stock using the following formula:

Formula: $\frac{\text{Investment Value}}{\text{Price Per Share}} = \text{\# of Shares}$ **Example:** $\frac{\$2000.00}{\$39.98} = 50.02 \text{ shares}$

5. Record the number of shares you were able to purchase in the Number of Shares column. (Do not round answers. Drop all numbers beyond the hundredth place.)

Tracking Table

Stock	Price Per Share	Number of Shares	Value of Individual Stock Investment
			$
			$
			$
			$
			$
		Total Portfolio Value	$

Week Four Steps: Complete your second tracking table. Use the names of the stock and the number of shares you purchased from week one. Use the financial page of a major newspaper or the Internet to locate each stock's present price per share. Then calculate the value of each individual stock investment.

What is the total portfolio value? ______________________________

Did you earn or lose money over the four weeks? ______________________________

Answer Keys

Constructed Response answers will vary but suggested answers have been included.

Unit 1: Financial vs. Economic Literacy
Assessment (p. 3)
Matching:
1. D 2. E 3. B 4. C 5. A

Fill in the Blanks:
6. bought, sold 7. products
8. teachers, cooks, bankers
9. raw 10. money, time

Constructed Response:
Because resources are scarce or limited, individuals, businesses, and nations will never have all they want of goods and services.

Knowledge Builder (p. 4)
1. National economy is the way in which the things people want and need are made, sold, and used within a particular country. Global economy is the way in which the things people want and need are made, sold, and used around the world.
2. Financial literacy is understanding and effectively using money management skills. Economic literacy is understanding the way in which the things people want and need are made, sold, and used in a country.
3. Saving is money you set aside for future use. Investing is putting money into something that will make a profit over time.

Unit 2: Making Financial Decisions
United States Money
Assessment (p. 6)
Matching:
1. D 2. E 3. A 4. B 5. C

True or False:
6. T
7. F: Coins are produced by the United States Mint. Bills are produced by the Bureau of Engraving and Printing.
8. F: The 100-dollar bill is the largest bill printed in the United States.
9. T
10. F: The first U.S. paper money was issued during the American Revolution.

Constructed Response:
The $5, $10, $20, $50, and $100 bills have been redesigned. Because of their high value, several security features have been incorporated into the design of these bills. This makes the bills more difficult to counterfeit.

Knowledge Builder (p. 7)
1. Abraham Lincoln, Lincoln Memorial (also Lincoln scenes and shield)
2. Thomas Jefferson, Monticello (also Lewis & Clark scenes)
3. Franklin D. Roosevelt, Torch and sprigs of laurel and oak
4. George Washington, Eagle (recent series vary featuring states, parks, women)
5. John F. Kennedy, Presidential Seal

Knowledge Builder (p. 8)
1. George Washington, The Great Seal
2. Abraham Lincoln, Lincoln Memorial
3. Alexander Hamilton, U.S. Treasury
4. Andrew Jackson, The White House
5. Ulysses S. Grant, U.S. Capitol
6. Benjamin Franklin, Independence Hall

Knowledge Builder (p. 9)
Teacher check

Money Math
Assessment (p. 12)
Multiple Choice:
1. C 2. B 3. A 4. C

Question/Answer:
5. $1.70 6. $3.85

Budgeting
Assessment (p. 14)
1. A budget is a plan for spending your money.
2. Needs are things you need to survive such as food. Wants are things you would like to have but are not needed for survival such as a bicycle.
3. A change in need, income, or an emergency
4. Rent and car payments
5. Groceries and entertainment
6. $50, $30, $20

Knowledge Builder (p. 15)
Teacher check

Knowledge Builder (p. 16)
Teacher check

Smart Shopping
Assessment (p. 18)
1. $0.66 2. $0.52 3. $0.90
4. Best Buy

Constructed Response:
HTTPS is secure, but HTTP is not secure, misspelling for dog in website address, used .co instead of .com

Knowledge Builder (p. 19)
Teacher check

Knowledge Builder (p. 20)
Teacher check

Discounts and Coupons
Assessment (p. 22)
1. F: A sales discount is the amount or percentage the regular price of an item or service is lowered.
2. T
3. Sales discount: $1.20, Sale price: $6.80
4. Sales discount: $5.00, Sale price: $10.00

Constructed Response:
Coupons and discount codes can be used to redeem special discounts and deals, in-store or online. A coupon is a small piece of paper that allows you to get a service or product for free or at a lower price. Coupons are also available online. A discount code is made up of random letters and numbers that often appear on coupons or on retailers' websites. When the code is entered at checkout, the discount is applied to the price.

Knowledge Builder (p. 23)
Teacher check

Knowledge Builder (p. 24)
Teacher check

Sales Receipts
Assessment (p. 26)
Multiple Choice:
1. B 2. C 3. D 4. C

Fill in the Blanks:
5. $40.44; $42.87 6. $36.08, $13.92

Knowledge Builder (p. 27)
1. Sports and More
2. 405 East Street, Greenfield, NY 12833
3. Sam West 4. Kate Jones
5. (615) 555-0109 6. 07/22/2024, 1:59
7. 2678 8. T-shirt
9. 2 10. $22.72
11. $45.44 12. $5.00
13. $2.43 14. $42.87
15. credit card 16. 45AV182
17. Exchange and refund within 10 days with original receipt

Knowledge Builder (p. 28)
Hamburger Palace:
Subtotal: $18.95, Total: $20.63
Tip: 15% Tip $2.84, Total $21.79
18% Tip $3.41, Total $22.36
20% Tip $3.79, Total $22.74
Tip: (Excellent 20%) $3.79
Total: $24.42
Pizza Delight:
Subtotal: $74.26
Total: $77.39
Change: $22.61
Tip: $11.14

Unit 3: The Economy
Ups and Downs in the Economy
Assessment (p. 30)
Matching:
1. E 2. C 3. B 4. A 5. D

Fill in the Blanks:
6. growing 7. inflation
8. expanding 9. less, save
10. decrease

Constructed Response:
People are forced to pay more for goods and services, so they are able to buy less. People become cautious about spending money.

Knowledge Builder (p. 31)

Expansion is a time when business is booming. New businesses are opening. There are lots of jobs for people, wages are high, and the unemployment rate is low. People have extra money; they buy new houses and new cars, go on trips to other countries, and invest in the stock market. People can borrow money from banks at low interest rates because they have a steady income.

Slowdown is a time when businesses are still operating in a healthy way, but they stop hiring new employees. Slowly the banks start increasing the interest rates on loans. People start to think twice about buying a house or a new car. The prices of some items in the grocery store begin to increase. The price of stock on the stock market begins to drop. People begin to be cautious about spending money.

Recession usually occurs when some major event happens, such as a stock market crash, a war, a major pandemic, or a natural catastrophe like a hurricane or drought. The interest on bank loans skyrockets. Businesses can't sell their products because people are afraid to spend money. Businesses start to lay off their workers and close their doors. People lose their homes because they are no longer employed. If the recession lasts too long, it can become a depression.

Recovery is the time it takes for a country to come out of a recession or depression. Usually, the government will initiate programs to help individuals and companies get started again, and slowly, people start to find jobs. The government can also pay for some employees' salaries to encourage companies to hire. The banks are forced to lower the interest rates on loans.

Knowledge Builder (p. 32)

1. Expansion/Recovery
2. Expansion/Recovery
3. Recession
4. Recovery
5. Recession
6. Expansion
7. Recession
8. Slowdown
9. Expansion
10. Recovery

Inflation and Deflation
Assessment (p. 34)

1. Goods and services are in high demand.
2. Too many goods and services are available and there is not enough money in circulation to purchase those goods or pay for the services.
3. Prices increase, but their income does not. They spend more of their income on necessities such as food, gas, and rent.
4. Creeping inflation because prices rise slowly.
5. Walking inflation is 3% to 10% a year.
6. The inflation rate is more than 10% a year. Prices rise quickly. Wages can't keep up with rising costs.

Knowledge Builder (p. 35)

Inflation:

1. Demand = 4, Supply = 3
2. too much
3. up
4. Increased demand drives prices up.
5. down

Deflation:

6. Demand = 2, Supply = 3
7. too little
8. down
9. Because demand decreases, there is a fall in the overall level of prices.
10. up

Knowledge Builder (p. 36)

1. Ham and Cheese Sandwich, Turkey Club Sandwich, Roast Beef Sandwich, French Fries, Giant Cookie, Soda
2. Soda
3. Grilled Cheese Sandwich, Potato Chips, Fresh Fruit Cup, Milk, and Lemonade
4. Lemonade
5. $9.40; $7.50; inflation

Unit 4: Taxes
Financing the Government
Assessment (p. 38)

Matching:

1. E 2. A 3. C 4. B 5. D

Fill in the Blanks:

6. Internal Revenue Service
7. Property
8. Medicare
9. Income
10. Social Security

Constructed Response:

The money collected from taxes is used for public services that benefit all people living in the United States or in a certain state or city. The revenue from the taxes is used for such things as public schools, police protection, public libraries, community centers, and parks. Examples of expenses are salaries of elected officials, such as the president, members of Congress, and public employees such as police. The government must pay for public goods and services it provides to citizens. Public goods and services include national defense, public health services, road improvements, libraries, parks, and education.

Knowledge Builder (p. 39–40)
Teacher check

Payday
Assessment (p. 42)
Multiple Choice:
1. D 2. D 3. C 4. C 5. C
6. B

Constructed Response:

Gross income is the amount of money a person makes before deductions are taken out. Net income is gross income minus all the taxes and other deductions. This is what is known as take-home pay. To ensure you have enough money to cover your necessary monthly expenses, it's helpful to base your monthly budget on net income, not gross income.

Knowledge Builder (p. 43)
1. $600
2. $31,200
3. Federal Tax = $72.00
   State Tax = $29.70
   Social Security Tax = $37.20
   Medicare Tax = $8.70
4. $452.40

Knowledge Builder (p. 44)
1. $490.00 2. $379.25
3. none 4 $12.25
5. Federal Tax = $49.00
   Social Security Tax = $7.11
   Medicare Tax = $30.38
   State Tax = $24.26
6. Gross income is the amount of money Jane makes before deductions are taken out. Net income is less because it is Jane's gross income minus all the taxes and other deductions.

Income Tax
Assessment (p. 46)
1. Gross income is the amount of money a person makes before deductions are taken out. Net income is gross income minus all the taxes and other deductions. This is what is known as take-home pay.
2. If the taxpayer's total tax payments are greater than the total tax due, they receive a refund from the government.
3. The W-2 form is used by employees to complete individual tax returns. Among other things, it includes the total amount of income earned and the amount of federal income tax withheld over the given year.
4. The IRS may levy (seize) assets such as wages and bank accounts plus your property including your car, boat, or home.
5. Taxpayers are responsible for accurately reporting all their income and filing the 1040 form on time. Taxpayers are legally responsible for preparing and submitting a tax return to the Internal Revenue Service by April 15th of each year.
6. Employers are required to withhold income tax payments from your paychecks. Employers prepare a W-2 form for each employee and send a copy to the employee as well as the IRS and the Social Security Administration.

Knowledge Builder (p. 47–48)
Teacher check

Checking
Assessment (p. 50)
Fill in the Blanks:
1. expenses 2. register
3. Online banking 4. overdraft

Multiple Choice:
5. C 6. C 7. A 8. A

Constructed Response:

The advantage of having a checking account is the ability to safely store money you intend to spend, either through debit card transactions, checks, or cash withdrawals.

The disadvantages are that checking accounts typically don't pay interest, and if you overdraw your account, you are charged a penalty.

Knowledge Builder (p. 51)

Date: Teacher check
Name: Teacher check
Account Number: 1234567
Cash: $15.00
Check Number: #7439, Amount: $103.00
Check Number: #202, Amount: $20.00
Subtotal: $138.00
Total: $138.00

Knowledge Builder (p. 52)

Check:
Date: October 19, 2025 (or any date before)
Pay to the Order of: PhoneTel Company $89.24
Dollars: Eighty-nine dollars and 24/100
Memo: Phone bill
Signature: Student's name
Check Register:
Check Number: 213
Date: 10/19
Description of Transaction: PhoneTel Company
Payment: $89.24
Balance: $335.68

Debit Cards

Assessment (p. 54)

Multiple Choice:
1. C 2. C 3. A 4. B 5. A
6. B

Constructed Response:

A digital wallet is an app that stores your debit card payment information and allows you to make electronic transactions using such devices as your cell phone, smartwatch, laptop, tablet, and computer. The transaction information is electronically transferred to your bank.

Knowledge Builder (p. 55)

1. Bank Well
2. Carrie Clark
3. Where the payment network logos indicate debit cards are accepted
4. Call the card's customer service number or visit website
5. 10/28
6. 0123 4567 8910 1112
7. Security feature that helps prevent fraud and counterfeiting

Knowledge Builder (p. 56)

1. Middle State Bank, 411 North Street, My Town, MI 55555
2. Sue Tompson
3. 0012300123004567
4. Cardholder used it at the ATM
5. T-shirt Palace
6. The beginning balance is the total amount of money in the account on March 27. The ending balance is the amount in the account on April 25, including all debits and credits. More money has been deposited than withdrawn.

Savings

Assessment (p. 58)

True or False:
1. F: Some banks require a minimum deposit to open a savings account.
2. F: Some banks charge fees associated with a savings account.
3. T
4. F: Most savings accounts earn interest, but the rate can vary.
5. T
6. T
7. F: The FDIC is an insurance company that protects the savings and checking accounts of bank depositors.

Constructed Response:

Easy access to funds, ability to earn interest, federally insured, requires little or no money to open an account, earns interest

Knowledge Builder (p. 59)

1 year: $5.00, $105.00
2 years: $5.25, $110.25
3 years: $5.51, $115.76
4 years: $5.79, $121.55

Knowledge Builder (p. 60)

Teacher check

Loans

Assessment (p. 62)

1. A loan is a contract between a borrower and a lender. The borrower promises to repay the lender in a certain amount of time.
2. The interest rate is the fee charged for borrowing the money, shown as a percentage of the principal.
3. The loan payment schedule tells the borrower when to start paying on the loan, how often to make payments, and the minimum (lowest) payment amount required.
4. A term loan is a loan where a fixed amount of money is borrowed for a specified period of time.
5. Failure to pay on time could lead to the borrower being fined, taken to court, or jail.
6. *Loan Payment Schedule:*
   Month 1: Principal: $180.63
   Month 2: Payment: $209.80
   Month 3: Beginning Balance: $6,637.98
   Month 4: Ending Balance: $6,272.94

Knowledge Builder (p. 63)

Down Payment and Loan Total:

	Car #1	Car #2	Car #3
10% Down Payment:	$1,200	$1,700	$2,500
Amount of Bank Loan:	$10,800	$15,300	$22,500

Monthly Payment:
Car #1: Monthly Payment = $305.56
Car #2: Monthly Payment = $375.00
Car #3: Monthly Payment = $333.33

Knowledge Builder (p. 64)

Teacher check

Credit Cards

Assessment (p. 66)

Matching:
1. D 2. C 3. B 4. A

Question/Answer:

5. Interest is a fee charged by the lender for borrowing money.
6. When they don't pay the balance on the card in full each month
7. They are borrowing money from the business that issued the card.
8. They are security features that help prevent fraud and counterfeiting.

Constructed Response:

Advantage: convenience; allows you to buy now and pay later. Disadvantage: If a loan is not paid by the due date, interest charges are added to the balance.

Knowledge Builder (p. 67)

1. $4,392.31 2. $1,317.44 3. $1,000.00
4. $117.00 5. $13,700.00 6. $72.96
7. May 24, 2025
8. Michael will pay more interest, and it will take longer to pay off the balance.

Knowledge Builder (p. 68)

Teacher check

Investment

Assessment (p. 70)

Matching:
1. E 2. B 3. D 4. C 5. A

Multiple Choice:
6. A 7. A 8. C 9. D

Constructed Response:

Saving is for emergencies and short-term goals. A savings account is protected by the FDIC. Investing is for long-term money growth. Investments often involve a certain amount of risk. The investor can lose all of their investment.

Knowledge Builder (p. 71)

1. The YTD column indicates the stock increased in value 28.80% over the year. The Chg column indicates the stock's price increased $0.35 that trading day.
2. The YTD column indicates the stock decreased in value 61.70 % over the year.

Knowledge Builder (p. 72)

Teacher check